D1084648

The Second World War's Military Legacy

The Second World War's Military Legacy

The Atomic Bomb and Much More

David Wragg

Pen & Sword
MILITARY

First published in Great Britain in 2014 by
PEN & SWORD MILITARY
an imprint of
Pen & Sword Books Ltd
47 Church Street
Barnsley
South Yorkshire
S70 2AS

ISBN 978-1-78159-318-9

Typeset by Concept, Huddersfield, West Yorkshire, HD4 5JL.
Printed and bound in England by CPI Group (UK) Ltd, Croydon CR0 4YY.

Pen & Sword Books Ltd incorporates the imprints of Pen & Sword Archaeology, Atlas, Aviation, Battleground, Discovery, Family History, History, Maritime, Military, Naval, Politics, Railways, Select, Social History, Transport, True Crime, and Claymore Press, Frontline Books, Leo Cooper, Praetorian Press, Remember When, Seaforth Publishing and Wharncliffe.

For a complete list of Pen & Sword titles please contact
PEN & SWORD BOOKS LIMITED
47 Church Street, Barnsley, South Yorkshire, S70 2AS, England
E-mail: enquiries@pen-and-sword.co.uk
Website: www.pen-and-sword.co.uk

Contents

List of Plates

A replica of the next of Hitler's *Vergeltungswaffen*, the V2, the first ballistic missile.

A Trident missile launched from a submarine breaks from the sea.

The first surface-to-air guided missile (SAM) to become operational was the American Nike Ajax, shown here on a launcher.

A cutaway drawing showing the interior of a typical turbofan engine, developed from the early turbojets of the Second World War.

A wartime shot of trials with the Sikorsky R-4 helicopter, with Igor Sikorsky himself sitting with his left leg out of the cockpit.

Contemporary helicopters such as the AgustaWestland Wildcat, developed from the earlier Lynx, are fast and can carry anti-submarine torpedoes or anti-shipping missiles.

The British contribution to interceptors was the English Electric, later British Aircraft Corporation (BAC), Lightning which could climb to 40,000 feet in just three minutes and fly at twice the speed of sound.

Interdiction bombing: a General Dynamics F-111 shown dropping Mk 82 bombs.

A Douglas C-47, known to the British as the Dakota and to the Americans as the Skytrain, dropping supplies over Burma.

The largest Allied glider in operational service was the Hamilcar, seen here from above with its nose doors open and a vehicle trail running away from the glider.

Search and rescue (SAR): a department within RAF Fighter Command provided airborne SAR using aircraft such as the Supermarine Walrus, seen here on trials.

Four-wheel-drive vehicles: a Willys Jeep with US troops in the North African desert.

The British Land-Rover, a wider and more stable vehicle than the original Jeep, led in turn to the Range Rover and what has become known as the SUV or 'sport utility vehicle'.

The first truly successful amphibious vehicle was the American DUKW, pronounced 'duck': this one is shown crossing the Rhine.

Most tanks were still landed ashore from Landing Craft, Tank (LCTs) as seen here with a British Crusader tank.

RFA *Mounts Bay*, a landing ship dock (LSD) currently in service with the Royal Fleet Auxiliary

A cutaway drawing showing the interior of a typical landing platform dock (LPD); in this case the US navy's *San Antonio* class.

The French *Colbert*, a modern stealth frigate with the radar image of a fishing vessel.

The RFA *Fort Victoria*, one of the Royal Fleet Auxiliary's most modern ships with a 'one-stop' fuel and stores replenishment service.

The *Sandown*-class minehunter, HMS *Ramsay*.

HMS *Daring*, one of the Royal Navy's Type 45 air-defence destroyers.

Introduction

In looking at the world before and after the Second World War, it is clear that it had changed a great deal. Of course, the same can be said about the world before and after the First World War. For a start, the post-war world was far less stable, mainly due to the shock that the Bolshevik Revolution in Russia sent through the rest of Europe. One can argue that the seeds of the Second World War were sown in the First World War and in the decisions enforced afterwards by the victors.

There were certainly equally great political and social changes after the Second World War. On this occasion it was China that changed to communism, while much of Eastern Europe was occupied by Soviet troops and governments favourable to the USSR were installed. Elsewhere, the nations of Western Europe started to disband their empires, with widely varying degrees of success and different approaches adopted by the United Kingdom, France, The Netherlands, Spain and Portugal.

Yet it is the technological changes to the armed forces that concern us here, especially those that had their origins in the way the armed forces adapted to developments in warfare. Anyone today who was transported by time machine back to 1938 would have found a much different place. No television outside the London area; no mobile telephones; even difficulty in getting a land-line, with contact once one was provided often entailing using a manually-operated switchboard. There was no colour printing in newspapers. Motor cars were much less commonplace and motorways either scarce, or in the case of the UK, non-existent. Steam ruled on most of the surface railways, although displaced by electric trains underground; the Southern Railway was among the main exceptions, having electrified its suburban network and its busiest main lines. Long-distance travel was usually by sea using ocean liners or, also rare these days, using a cargo ship that carried a small number of passengers.

In short, it was a greyer, dirtier, slower and altogether less convenient world. There were few 'convenience' foods and takeaway mainly meant fish and chips, with one or two regional variations. Communication was much poorer. Cars, long-distance travel and indeed, much travel to foreign parts, were all things that were limited to the wealthy few.

Many of the 'improvements' that we take for granted today, and which not everyone might agree were an improvement, came from the war years and the military adoption and adaptation of the new, the untried and often untested. Widespread car ownership and the proliferation of mobile phones and colour televisions had little to do with this, or at least the connection is tenuous. However, long-distance air travel that is affordable and indeed, the idea of air travel for all, is something that owes much to the war years when many were introduced to air travel while in the military.

There are other such examples. The use of the helicopter for disaster relief, as an air ambulance or an aid to policing is something that can be traced back to the war years, although then the main uses were seen primarily as being military.

The technological list is long. It includes nuclear weapons – which many argue preserved peace during the chilly years of the Cold War – and their means of delivery, including cruise missiles and ballistic missiles. Of course, others will argue that nuclear weapons are an evil and that the world is less safe today because of their presence. Some would say that the reason why the world is less safe is that the old certainties of the Cold War have gone and nuclear weapons are no longer confined to nations led by logical leaders anxious to preserve their countries and their peoples but available to others who set their beliefs above safety and before security.

I once read that aviation – i.e. heavier-than-air flight – made more progress during the four years or so of the First World War than would have been possible in fifty years of peacetime development. That such progress was spurred on by the demands of war is beyond doubt, although I would question the 'fifty years' as there was much more progress in aviation before the outbreak of war than many people realize, with features such as monocoque construction of aircraft and even work on retractable undercarriages, while in pre-revolutionary Russia Igor Sikorsky produced an aeroplane that was described as the first 'airbus'.

Indeed, much that seemed new in the First World War was already well-established elsewhere, with the predecessor of the machine gun, barbed wire and trench warfare all having come from the American Civil War fifty years earlier. Even so, there were genuine advances, of which the most notable were the battle tank and the aircraft carrier. There were also missed, or perhaps one should say bungled, opportunities: the development of amphibious warfare that was first intended to see a direct invasion of Germany on the coast of Pomerania, followed by a march on Berlin to end the war and then by an attempt to ease the pressure on the Western and Eastern Fronts by an invasion of Gallipoli.

Essentially it is to the Second World War that we must look for the significant developments that remain with us today. There are many to choose from.

First of all, however, we must place developments in their proper context. In-flight refuelling was developed before the Second World War but not for military purposes as it was a means of extending the range of the Short Empire flying boats being used on Imperial Airways' services and in particular enabling these aircraft to fly across the North Atlantic.

Paratroops were an innovation in the Soviet Union between the wars and so while used offensively for the first time in the Second World War, they were not a wartime invention. Not only that, the post-war history of the use of paratroops has been patchy. They were used in French Indo-China, at Suez and in the Congo but increasingly they were pushed out by the helicopter which, despite its relatively slow speed, short range and limited carrying capacity, has a proven ability to get troops to where they are needed with fewer casualties than a parachute drop. If that was not enough, it can get them out again! During the Normandy landings, one battalion of paratroops suffered 40 per cent casualties and not all through enemy action. The truth is, in fact, that paratroops were a high risk element in the Second World War. For the Germans, the invasion of Crete was costly; so costly that Hitler for a while forbade any further airborne assaults. Had the British troops defending Crete not lost their heavy weapons including anti-aircraft guns and their communications equipment in the evacuation from Greece, the Germans might have failed. As it was, despite losing control of the air, the British still had control of the seas and the German seaborne invasion was virtually wiped out by the Mediterranean Fleet.

Amphibious assault is not new and in Europe dates from the Battle of Marathon in 490 BC but the big difference that came in the Second World War was the invention of the landing craft and landing ship, making amphibious assault much easier and more efficient.

The use of artillery rockets became widespread during the Second World War, not only with the devastating fire of the Soviet 'Stalin Organs' on the Eastern Front but also with landing craft modified to fire artillery rockets and used in the Normandy landings. Yet these also pre-date the war, having been introduced to Europe by Sir William Congreve in 1805 and then used by the Royal Navy during the Second Battle of Copenhagen in 1807. That battle also brought us the concept of 'collateral damage' with very high civilian casualties. In fact, so-called collateral damage might be new to the residents of the British Isles but the Americans came face-to-face with it when caught up in the civil war and it was well-known in many other countries that had wars fought on their territory in the centuries before.

Sonar dated from between the world wars, when it was known by the acronym ASDIC, reflecting the work of the Anglo-French Allied Submarine Detection Investigation Committee. It is a system that is in widespread use today but not every navy had this in 1939 and it was a massive improvement over the First World War use of hydrophones for submarine detection. However, it was not just its use alone that helped fight submarines but also systems such as 'Hedgehog' that fired anti-submarine weapons so that they exploded clear of the ship. Earlier anti-submarine ships had needed to be fast to escape being badly damaged by their own depth-charges. So improvements in anti-submarine warfare are worth including here.

Today's airliners can land in all but the worst visibility and in conditions that would have grounded flights not so long ago. This is thanks to automatic landing systems. In the Second World War, the Royal Air Force used a system called FIDO, an acronym for 'Fog Investigation and Dispersal Operation', although the RAF later claimed that it stood for 'Fog, Intensive, Dispersal of'. Yet this was not the predecessor of today's automatic landing systems, which originated with one called 'autoland', first employed on a Hawker Siddeley Trident and which used computers to land the aircraft safely. FIDO was much more basic, using petrol burners on either side of the runway. Not something that any responsible aviation safety authority would allow and certainly not a direct link to the systems used by modern aircraft.

Radar was also invented before the war but not long before and this made a massive difference, not just in air defence but also in improving navigation, especially of Allied bombers on night raids whose ability to hit the target in the early days was extremely limited.

Of course, one of the big features of the Second World War was the way in which the war in the Far East was brought to an end much sooner than anticipated by the use of nuclear weapons. Many might not see the availability of nuclear weapons, and now even more powerful thermonuclear weapons, as a welcome legacy but to Allied prisoners of war and the nationals of Japanese-occupied territory, not to mention the millions of Japanese who were suffering from starvation towards the end of the war and the countless millions who would have suffered in an Allied invasion, this was a blessing.

In the V1 rocket, one can see the precursor of the cruise missile, and in the V2, the precursor of the ballistic missile.

While we are looking at the military legacy, much of what appeared has assumed considerable importance even in civilian life. The jet engine brought reliability to aircraft engines and played an important part in making air travel not just faster but also more affordable. Four-wheel-drive vehicles are no longer the preserve of the military; indeed, in the developed world the numbers in civilian use outnumber those belonging to the military. The helicopter is not an exotic piece of military equipment but is now commonplace in civilian use.

The Second World War's military legacy is a long one but includes much that is worthwhile. Recalling the lack of cohesion among British, French, Belgian and Dutch forces in May and June 1940, it is also worth bearing in mind that one lesson learned was not just that military alliances were essential but that it was also important to exercise together and learn how to operate collaboratively.

The use of Special Forces became more common during the Second World War and often included the work of combined operations; while on the home front bomb disposal became essential and sadly has grown in importance over the years that followed.

SECTION ONE

GENERAL

Chapter 1

Nuclear Weapons

The potential development of an atomic bomb was recognized before the Second World War and research was carried out separately in the United States and the United Kingdom. Scientists warned the American government of the potential of 'extremely powerful bombs of a new type' and on 2 August 1939, Albert Einstein wrote to President Franklin D. Roosevelt urging that he investigate the possibility of a plutonium bomb. Work in the United States was carried out initially under the code name of the 'Development of Substitute Materials', while that in the United Kingdom was code-named 'Tube Alloys'. Initially, the UK was ahead of the USA but as a result of the British government's initial refusal to share its research, the USA took the lead in the project. However, after the Quebec Conference of 1943, work proceeded with British and Canadian involvement.

The United Kingdom was ahead in its research but lacked the manpower and finance to handle the project, which in the end required 129,000 personnel, of whom almost three-quarters were construction workers. A site for a suitable testing ground would have been impossible to find in the British Isles. In the end, the project cost US$2 billion or, at current prices, US$26 billion.

Work started in 1939 but the pace increased from 1942. The code name was first changed to the 'Manhattan District' and then to the 'Manhattan Project'. Work took place over a number of locations, mainly across the United States but also in British Columbia.

Two types of nuclear weapon were developed, both using nuclear fission. The simpler version was the 'gun type', in which conventional explosive fired a uranium 'bullet' into a uranium 'target', and the more complicated was the 'implosion type', using explosives to compress fissile material such as plutonium into an increasingly dense sphere. The implosion type was regarded as being more powerful but more difficult to manufacture and the resulting bomb had a much larger circumference.

Despite severe shortages of suitable materials, it was decided to conduct a live detonation and a site was chosen at the Alamogordo Army Air Force Field in New Mexico, close to the Los Alamos laboratories where much of the development work was handled. The live test was known as 'Trinity' and used an implosion-type bomb nicknamed the 'Gadget' dropped from a steel tower 100 feet (just over 31m) high at 0530 hours on 16 July 1945. The bomb had an explosion force calculated as equivalent to 20 kilotons of TNT. It left a layer of radioactive glass, later known as 'Trinitite', in the desert that was 250 feet (77m) wide and the shock wave could be felt more than 100 miles (161km) away, while the mushroom cloud rose to a height of 7.5 miles (12km). As the explosion could be heard as far away as El Paso in Texas, a statement had to be released reporting an explosion at the air base.

From this time onwards, the explosive power of nuclear and thermo-nuclear weapons has been calculated in kilotons, each equivalent to 1,000 tons of TNT, or megatons, a million tons of TNT.

Two bombs were manufactured and ready for use by August, while further bombs were under construction so that a third atomic bomb would have been available had Japan not surrendered. The first bomb was of the gun type, was called 'Little Boy' and was used against Hiroshima on 6 August 1945, while the second bomb used the implosion method, was known as 'Fat Man' and was dropped on Nagasaki on 9 August.

Finding a suitable aircraft was the next problem. The ideal aircraft would have been the British Avro Lancaster, which had been used by the Royal Air Force to drop a wide variety of heavy or unusual munitions including the 22,000lb 'Grand Slam' earthquake bomb and the mines known as 'Upkeep' used against the Ruhr dams. However, this would have created problems regarding maintenance, security and pilot train-ing, so modified versions of the Boeing B-29 Superfortress were used, with the two bomb bays combined into one. Both atomic bomb missions were given to the USAAF's 393rd Bombardment Squadron.

Suitable targets were already becoming fewer as the result of increas-ingly intensive raids with incendiary bombs over Japanese cities. For the first bomb, Hiroshima was chosen as it was an important port and a major army depot. Nagasaki was the alternative should poor visibility make a successful attack on Hiroshima doubtful. The plane, named *Enola Gay* after the pilot's mother, was flown by Colonel Paul Tibbets of the USAAF. Final assembly of the bomb was completed in the air to avoid any prob-lems during take-off. It was detonated at 1,750 feet and the blast was esti-mated as being equivalent to 13 kilotons, killing between 70,000 and 80,000 people immediately and wounding as many more, while an area of more than 4 square miles was devastated, destroying almost 70 per cent of the city's buildings.

The next target was intended to be Kokura but low cloud made accurate bombing difficult and after flying over the target the bomber, commanded by Major Charles Sweeney, headed for Nagasaki. The second bomb was an implosion type and was aimed at the industrial areas of the city located in the Urakami Valley. Because of the valley terrain, the death toll was lower than at Hiroshima with 35,000 killed, 60,000 wounded and 44 per cent of the city's buildings destroyed in the 21-kiloton blast.

Post-war, the United States continued testing, including tests to assess the damage that nuclear weapons would have on warships. The Soviet Union was the next nation to test a nuclear weapon, having become aware through its spies during the war that a new weapon was being developed. The United Kingdom followed and was later joined as a nuclear power by France and then China. In more recent years India, Pakistan and North Korea have also developed nuclear weapons, while Israel is believed to have them. South Africa had developed a nuclear capability at one stage but has since become the only nation to abandon such weapons. When the USSR broke up, many of its weapons were based in the Ukraine and these too have been removed.

Not all the applications for the power of the atom were military. Many peacetime uses were also envisaged, including using nuclear explosions for construction work, but the radioactive fallout prevented this from happening. Work on nuclear-powered rocket engines also failed to produce workable results. The one area in which the atom has been put to work has been electricity generation; even countries not armed with nuclear weapons are now operating nuclear power stations.

The next stage was the development of a fusion weapon, more usually known as the hydrogen bomb because it uses isotopes of hydrogen to achieve nuclear fusion. Nuclear fusion has little radioactive fallout but fusion bombs, or H-bombs, are far from being completely 'clean' as they initially require nuclear fission to achieve fusion. The only nations with H-bombs are the United States, United Kingdom, Soviet Union, France and China, although India claims to have achieved nuclear fusion but some doubt that full fusion is in fact available to India. Nuclear power stations use nuclear fission and efforts to generate electricity from fusion have so far failed.

Other weapons uses have included such variants as the neutron bomb, intended to soak an area with radioactivity while leaving much of the infrastructure intact. Nuclear depth-bombs have also been developed to deal with fast-moving and deep-diving nuclear-powered submarines.

At first, nuclear weapons were intended to be dropped by bombers but the hazards of flying into well-defended enemy airspace and the difficulties facing the bomber crews in returning to base resulted in stand-off weapons being developed so that these, usually rocket or jet-powered, could be discharged while some distance from the target. Increasingly, intercontinental ballistic missiles (ICBMs) became the favoured method of delivery and, while the first generation of these was land-based, the fact that the locations would become known and targeted by an enemy meant that submarine-launched missiles increasingly became the norm. The first was the United States navy's Polaris system which was also used by the Royal Navy and the current submarine-launched ICBM is Trident, again used by the United States and the Royal Navy. The Soviet Union (now Russia) and France also developed submarine-based ICBMs.

The importance of having missiles based aboard submarines, themselves nuclear-powered, has been twofold. First, the location of the submarines would be difficult to establish. Second, as a result of this, submarine-based weapons could be used even after the home country was devastated by a nuclear attack: this is the so-called 'second strike' capability, which is the ultimate deterrent.

At first, thermonuclear weapons grew in size with many 10-megaton warheads produced but the largest was a Soviet 50-megaton bomb, known officially as 'Big Ivan' but nicknamed the 'Tsar-Bomba' following the break-up of the Soviet Union. This was tested in the Soviet Arctic with impressive results but was far too big to be practical as its delivery presented problems and, because of the widespread damage, it was of limited use militarily. It has been estimated that such a bomb could wipe out almost all of the United Kingdom with damage suffered as far away as Eastern Europe, while a bomb of this magnitude dropped on Germany would inflict damage as far away as the borders of Russia. In the United States, there are only three areas that would justify the use of such a large bomb: the New York area, the Chicago area and Los Angeles.

It soon became apparent that smaller warheads would be more effective. Starting with an upgrade of Polaris, multiple independently-targeted re-entry vehicles (MIRVs) were developed so that a single missile could deploy several warheads, attacking a number of targets but also ensuring that even if an anti-missile system was deployed, at least some of the warheads would get through. Trident missiles include a number of MIRVs, usually up to eight, but also include many that are intended to act as decoys.

Nuclear artillery shells were also developed, as well as theatre ballistic missiles. When the Soviet Union updated its theatre missiles in the 1970s, the United States responded with the introduction of cruise missiles. Initially cruise missiles were fired from mobile launchers on land but later versions could be air-launched, launched from surface vessels or from submarines. Dimensions varied but the most practical were those that could be fired through torpedo tubes. Jet-powered surface- and subsurface-launched cruise missiles need a booster to achieve sufficient speed but generally fly at low level. Most cruise missiles, it must be stated, have conventional warheads.

The problem with nuclear weapons has been not so much the massive power but the radioactive fallout. Many of those present at Hiroshima and Nagasaki died years later from cancers and other illnesses caused by radioactivity and there have been similar cases among those present during post-war tests of A-bombs and H-bombs.

These consequences were known even during the early developmental stages and many of the scientists involved were unsure whether the new 'super bomb' was acceptable. During the 1950s, public protest against nuclear weapons became more common. The danger of a nuclear war starting by accident was another major concern.

In 1963 the USA, the UK, France and the USSR signed a Partial Test Ban Treaty, which was followed by a number of agreements until the 1996 Comprehensive Test Ban Treaty. The earlier 1968 Nuclear Non-Proliferation Treaty had as its main aim the prevention of nuclear weapons spreading to states that hitherto had not possessed them. It also planned an eventual end to all nuclear weapons.

What has happened is that atmospheric nuclear tests have stopped, which is a step forward. A complete end to nuclear weaponry is probably unrealistic as the effect was recognized by both sides of using even a fraction of the nuclear arsenals possessed by both sides in the Cold War that lasted from the end of the Second World War until the end of the Warsaw Pact and the break-up of the Soviet Union. The emerging concept of 'mutually assured destruction', known as 'MAD', did nevertheless inhibit all-out war. Some even argue that nuclear proliferation might mean more widespread peace, although it could be said that rather than a true peace it would be a nuclear stand-off in those parts of the world such as the Middle East where there are deep and ongoing tensions. This argument does, of course, assume the rationality of the leaders of both sides in a dispute.

Attempts have been made to reduce the number of warheads, including limiting each of the UK's Trident missiles to four active warheads. American scientists estimate that in 2012 there were 17,000 warheads stored worldwide with about a quarter counted as 'active', i.e. ready for use. However, many countries including the UK have not declared the number of warheads in their nuclear arsenal. It is also usual for nuclear-armed states not to clarify the circumstances in which such weapons would be used and navies with nuclear weapons do not declare on which warships these are carried. The idea is to keep a potential enemy guessing. It is believed that the UK has around 250 nuclear warheads.

Chapter 2

Alliances and Exercises

There is nothing new about alliances between sovereign states but what did emerge during the Second World War was the concept of lasting alliances and close collaboration, including the armed forces of different countries exercising and training together.

Alliances had existed in the ancient world. In 415–413 BC the Athenian trading post at Segesta in Sicily was threatened by Syracuse, which was an ally of Corinth at the time. Much later, the Christian countries of Western Europe combined in the great crusades to drive the Arabs from the Holy Land.

The oldest and most enduring alliance today dates from 1373 between England and Portugal, with England supplanted by the United Kingdom since 1800. The early years of the twentieth century saw the *entente cordiale* between France and the United Kingdom with both countries concerned about the growing power of a united Germany as well as concerns about Russia. At the time, the UK was also the guarantor of Belgian neutrality.

As war spread across Europe in August 1914, the British sent troops to France, as they would do again in September 1939. Nevertheless, at the outset of both these global conflicts, the armed forces of the two nations did not exercise together, even though on the second occasion all concerned had the benefit of the experience of the First World War and Belgium knew that it could not defend itself against a German invasion without British and French assistance. In the First World War the British and French, later joined by the Italians, were known as the 'Entente Powers', while the Germans and Austro-Hungarians were the 'Central Powers'; however, collaboration was far more piecemeal than was the case in the Second World War.

In the First World War, collaboration was minimal during the Gallipoli campaign with a half-hearted French diversionary attack on mainland Anatolia, while the Japanese sent some destroyers to the Mediterranean to ease the pressure on the British Mediterranean Fleet. During the Russian Civil War, while forces were deployed by the British at several points, the only combined operation was in the East. British, Canadian, US and

Japanese forces attempted to advance westwards but as the United States and the Japanese had their own agendas, the campaign was doomed.

It is possible to argue that without the fall of France in June 1940, the situation might not have changed very much during the Second World War, or at least not until the United States entered the war in December 1941. Having personnel from France, Belgium, The Netherlands, Poland, Norway and Denmark plus some Czechs all under British control changed the situation considerably, especially once governments in exile were formed. All of these, plus the armed forces from the dominions, were under British control and were welded into a cohesive Allied fighting force with various degrees of success.

The Axis Powers operated in a different way. Japan was a member but not one that could be coordinated because not only was the country far removed from Germany and Italy but the Allies retained control of the seas. At first, Hitler was an admirer of his Italian counterpart, Mussolini, but Italy's delay in joining Germany until 10 June 1940 imposed a strain on their relationship. Germany did, nevertheless, come to the rescue of the Italians in Yugoslavia and Greece, and also in North Africa. However, in the latter theatre, any pretence that the Axis was an alliance of equals ended, for when Rommel had difficulties with his Italian counterpart, the order from Berlin was that he was to take the decisions.

The Molotov-Ribbentrop Pact between Germany and the USSR in August 1939, ahead of the invasion of Poland, was short-lived and opportunistic. It could have bought breathing space for the USSR, had Stalin been prepared to recognize the inevitable and listen to the advice he was being given.

Nevertheless, the Germans did need their allies and were joined with them especially in the over-ambitious and ultimately ill-fated Operation BARBAROSSA, the invasion of the Soviet Union. Troops not only from Italy but also from Hungary and Romania and even non-belligerent Spain joined the Germans in the campaign, while air force units were also despatched to join the Luftwaffe.

One of the least successful groupings of the Second World War was the American, British, Dutch and Australian (ABDA) Command, a hastily-conceived response to the advancing Japanese after the fall of Singapore. There was a unified command staffed in proportion to the numbers provided by the participants rather than by ability or experience but there was no time for any joint exercise and there were serious communications difficulties. The alliance ended with the Battle of the Java Sea when ABDA's optimistically-named 'Combined Striking Force' was beaten by the Japanese, largely because they had air power and the Combined Striking Force did not.

In the Far East, many senior American officers didn't want British assistance but they were overruled and the British were accepted on the basis that they were to provide their own support facilities and not to expect assistance from the United States navy; a rule that was ignored by many other American officers so that in due course collaboration became the norm. The US navy also conducted joint raids with the Royal Navy over Sumatra so that the British could become used to joint operations and massed attack by aircraft from more than one aircraft carrier. Nevertheless, despite the eventual creation of a British Pacific Fleet that was stronger and better balanced than any sent to sea by the Royal Navy before or since, the Pacific War was American-led. Despite this, as the war moved ever closer to Japan, the British were able to retake their colonies.

In Europe and North Africa there was greater cohesion and sharing. The British had command at sea and, when Europe was invaded, in the air with the Supreme Allied Commander, General of the Army (equivalent to Field Marshal) Dwight Eisenhower, having as his deputy Air Chief Marshal (equivalent to a USAAF four-star general) Sir Arthur Tedder of the RAF. Admiral Sir Bertram Ramsay was in command of the naval part of Operation OVERLORD, itself so important that it had its own code name, Operation NEPTUNE, while Air Chief Marshal Sir Trafford Leigh-Mallory commanded the tactical air forces. The friction between Eisenhower and the senior British army officer, General Sir Bernard Montgomery (later Field Marshal the Viscount Montgomery of Alamein), was largely due to a clash of personalities and 'Monty's' arrogance.

Nevertheless, there was a joint command: Supreme Headquarters Allied Powers in Europe (SHAPE). The Royal Air Force and the United States Army Air Forces continued joint operations with the Combined Bomber Offensive.

The wartime alliance fractured as soon as the war ended, with the Soviet Union having used the advance on Germany to create a network of satellite states, all communist dictatorships. The Western democracies stood firm and created the North Atlantic Treaty Organization (NATO), while the Soviet Union manufactured its own Warsaw Pact. Although both alliances had a command structure, the Warsaw Pact forces in any one country were always commanded by a senior Russian officer, while those of NATO had commanders drawn from the host country. A number of joint ventures such as NATO Standing Force Atlantic and NATO Standing Force Channel were created, with ships drawn from the member states and command circulated among the contributing states. The Warsaw Pact ended in the early 1990s as democracy was revived in some of the member states and the Soviet Union broke up.

Far less successful were the Baghdad Pact, which became the Central Treaty Organization (CENTO) when Baghdad left the western sphere of influence, and the South-East Asia Treaty Organization (SEATO), neither of which had a command structure and both of which folded. One reason for the failure of SEATO was the British desire to withdraw from 'east of Suez', although heavily involved east of the eponymous canal ever since! SEATO has been replaced by an alliance between the United States and both Australia and New Zealand, while exercises are held by the United States not only with these countries but also with other important states in the region.

NATO continues to conduct exercises and also provides support for member states if they have a shortfall in capability. A joint airborne early warning fleet that augmented the fleets of the United States, United Kingdom and France has been followed by a joint heavy-lift air transport fleet. So strong is NATO's command structure that operations under the auspices of the United Nations in the former Yugoslavia were directed by NATO, which was also the vehicle for combined operations for the liberation of Kuwait in 1991 and in both Afghanistan and Iraq.

Clearly, lessons have been learned that date from the Allied participation in the Second World War but increasingly these seem to have been forgotten by some governments as European nations have been cutting defence expenditure, while the United States is switching its attention to the Pacific to contain an increasingly ambitious and belligerent Communist China.

Chapter 3

Radar

While early work on radar, originally an acronym for RAdio Detection And Ranging but now a common noun, pre-dates the Second World War by several decades, not only was this a new technology available during the war years that has since become even more important, it was also an advantage held by the British at the outset of war. The actual term 'radar' is supposed to have been coined in the United States around 1940.

The system works by a radar dish or antenna emitting pulses of radio waves or microwaves that bounce off any object they encounter; the object then returns part of the pulses' energy to a dish or antenna that is usually on the same location as the transmitter. The transmitter does not have to be static or ground-based but can be aboard a ship or an aircraft, or on a motor vehicle if mobility is required.

Ironically, the original discovery that radio waves could be reflected from solid objects was made in Germany in 1886 by Heinrich Hertz. In the decade that followed, there were also similar discoveries in Russia. It was not until 1904, again in Germany, that Christian Hülsmeyer used radio waves to detect the presence of metallic objects and was able to demonstrate the ability to find a ship in dense fog, although unable at that point to show its distance from the transmitter. He later obtained patents for his system, which he called the 'telemobiloscope'.

In the 1930s, researchers in many countries working independently developed the technology that led to the modern concept of radar. The French even managed to develop an obstacle-locating radio apparatus, which was installed on the transatlantic liner *Normandie* in 1935. The French system, and those developed in the Soviet Union at around the same time, used continuous wave operation and could not provide the performance of the pulses that are the basis of modern radar. Work on pulse-based systems was undertaken at this time in the United Kingdom, the United States and Germany.

The British already had an early warning air defence network based on large sound detectors, which was inaccurate and not always reliable. It gave little indication of the strength of an approaching formation of aircraft, their height or speed, and was also vague regarding direction.

Robert Watson-Watt had been heading an Air Ministry (the government department that sponsored the Royal Air Force) team working on radar research and development and the pace quickened after 1 September 1936 when he became the superintendent of the new Bawdsey Research Station, based near Felixstowe on the Suffolk coast. The outcome was the development of a network of aircraft detection and tracking systems along the east and south coasts of England, named Chain Home. This network was operational in time for the Battle of Britain, when it eliminated the need for standing fighter patrols and could alert squadrons on stand-by in good time for them to counter an approaching enemy formation and direct them towards it.

Meanwhile, radar began to be installed on major British warships, although the Germans also made progress on this front with warships of the *Kriegsmarine* equipped with radar including the battle-cruisers *Gneisenau* and *Scharnhorst*.

By 1940, the British had a system that worked well in daylight but still left them vulnerable to night attack and both the Royal Air Force and their opponents, the German Luftwaffe, concentrated on night bombing raids as daylight losses proved too costly. Attempts to use ground-based radar to direct fighters onto enemy aircraft rarely worked. There had been earlier attempts in 1938 to fit radar to a commercial airliner in the United States but this was for safety, detecting other aircraft or obstacles along the route being flown. Nevertheless, a lightweight airborne radar was soon developed and fitted to the Bristol Beaufighter, a capable twin-engine night-fighter used over the UK and Malta. Better still was its successor, the de Havilland Mosquito, and with its arrival the success rate against German night-bombers began to improve.

The Germans used radio beams transmitted from ground stations to direct their bombers to the target area, with another system, mainly on board the aircraft, to indicate the distance to releasing bombs over the target. The British became aware of what was happening and introduced 'beacons' of their own to bend the German beams, as well as using the crude device of starting fires in open countryside in the hope that the Luftwaffe aircraft would mistake these for cities on fire after an air-raid and drop their bombs on the fake 'target'. By the outbreak of the Second World War, most bombers and many civil airliners were fitted with radio direction-finders, giving the bearings of radio beacons on the ground. Airliners used the system by navigating from beacon to beacon, while for bomber pilots the beacons enabled them to find their way back to their base after a mission. This was an improvement and did much to ensure that airline services became more reliable; while good visibility was required for a safe landing, low cloud or bad weather en route became much less of a problem. Even so, the radio beacons became less reliable the further the distance from a beacon and simple direction-finding using the beacons was not possible when more than 200 miles away.

The Luftwaffe came up with a solution: *Knickebein*. This was available before the outbreak of war and for the first two-and-a-half years of war provided a succession of aids to navigation and bombing accuracy far superior to any available elsewhere. A ground transmitter radiated a *Lorenz* beam, which was in fact a double beam with one beam transmitting Morse dots and the other Morse dashes. When the beams overlapped, the combined beam produced a steadier and finer note than either of its constituent parts. The *Knickebein* transmitter was mounted on railway bogies running on a circular track so that it could be aligned in the required direction. A second transmitter was used to produce a second set of beams which crossed the first set at the point at which the bomb had to be released. Given that by 1940 the Luftwaffe was able to locate transmitters in Norway, The Netherlands and France, almost any target in the UK could be identified in this way and bombing accuracy was just over half a mile. No special training was necessary over and above the instrument training essential for night-flying. Even so, once the RAF discovered *Knickebein*, it was jammed and became useless.

Nevertheless, the Germans were not standing still and a more accurate system soon followed. This was *X-Gerat*, meaning simply 'X-apparatus'. This was provided for a specially-equipped bomber group with about thirty aircraft for precision night-bombing. Instead of two beams there were four, with one beam for the route to the target and three cross beams. A special clock was fitted aboard the aircraft. The distance between crossing the first beam and the second was 18.6 miles (30km) and on crossing the second beam, the navigator would start the bombing clock, with the third beam being another 9.3 miles (15km) further on. On crossing the third beam, the navigator would press a button that stopped the first hand on the clock and started the second hand, and when this caught up with the first hand, a pair of electrical contacts closed and the bombs were released automatically. On the night of 14 November 1940, for the raid on Coventry, the route beam originated in a ground station west of Cherbourg and the three cross beams came from stations to the south of Calais. Once again, when the RAF discovered *X-Gerat*, jammers were built to counter the system.

The Germans next introduced *Y-Gerat*, which needed just a single ground station. This also had the bomber flying along the beam but one that was far more complex than those used by the first two systems. The ground station kept an accurate track of the aircraft by emitting a second signal which was picked up by the aircraft and re-transmitted back to the ground station. As the aircraft approached the target, the ground station then ordered the crew to release the bombs. Once again, this was very effective until the RAF discovered what was going on, after which *Y-Gerat* proved easy to jam.

During the early years of the war, British bombing accuracy was poor, with many aircraft not coming within the target area. The first step for the RAF was a system known as GEE, introduced in early 1942. Three ground-based transmitters were used to generate a complex pattern of pulses in a predetermined order and a special receiver was fitted to aircraft so that the navigator could measure the differences in the time of reception of the pulses, enabling him to read off his position from a special map. Because the distances were greater, when on operations over Germany GEE could not match the accuracy of *Knickebein*, which used stations based in occupied territory. Then it was the turn of the Germans to start jamming.

Around a year later, the RAF had its first radar-based precision bombing system, OBOE, so-named because its pulses had a similar sound to the musical instrument. This system used two ground stations: one known as the 'cat' station tracking the aircraft as it flew along an arc of constant range that ran through the target and passed correction signals if the aircraft deviated from the arc; and the second, known as the 'mouse' station, measuring the range along the arc. When the aircraft reached the bomb-release point, a signal was broadcast. As with *Y-Gerat*, the aircraft carried repeater-transmitters which amplified both signals and returned them to the ground stations.

Over short ranges OBOE was extremely accurate but its weakness was that due to the curvature of the earth, its usefulness was confined to an area within a range of 280 miles of each of the ground stations. It could also only handle one bomber at a time during its bombing run, which could take up to ten minutes. Fortunately, an arc from the east coast of England took in the Ruhr industrial area. The usefulness of the device was also enhanced by fitting it to de Havilland Mosquito pathfinder aircraft so that they could mark the target for the main force of bombers. It also proved difficult to jam, especially when later versions used short wavelengths.

Improvements over OBOE were the British GEE-H and the American SHORAN (SHOrt RAnge Navigation) systems. These were similar to OBOE but the transmissions came from the aircraft, leaving the ground stations to repeat back the pulses, and this enabled scores of aircraft to be handled at the same time.

A weakness of both the British and German systems was the need to use ground transmitters, meaning that the curvature of the earth limited the distance over which accurate navigation was possible. The problem was more acute for the RAF as the Germans were able to base transmitters in occupied territory, much closer to the mainland of Great Britain than a base in Germany would have been, but when the RAF planned to carry the war to the enemy in Germany, it was at a marked disadvantage. What was needed was a system independent of ground stations.

The development of the cavity magnetron that appeared in early 1943 offered a solution, providing the basis of the H2S centimetric radar which was carried in the aircraft and scanned the terrain under it. The strongest echoes were sent by built-up areas and mountains and the weakest from water, with open countryside falling between these two extremes. The echoes were displayed on a cathode-ray tube and the result was good enough to be compared with maps. Initially, this heavy system could only be used in heavy bombers but development reduced the weight and it became possible to fit it into smaller aircraft. The best results were produced by coastal targets with a sharp contrast between the built-up area of the port and the water or by targets siding astride a river. H2S in three marks were fitted to RAF bombers and a few sets were supplied to the USAAF for B-17s and B-24s. Meanwhile the Americans developed their own version, the H2X, which was eventually available in quantity and proved useful for bombing when the target areas were obscured by cloud. In 1944 a new development, the APS-20, was introduced for the USAAF's B-29 Superfortress bombers and this was the best wartime ground-mapping radar. The German equivalent appeared too late to be used operationally.

Other airborne radars were fitted to carrier-borne aircraft to enable them to hunt submarines at night or in low cloud, with even the obsolescent Fairey Swordfish biplane so equipped.

Meanwhile, on the ground anti-aircraft systems were improved by having searchlights guided by radar and then anti-aircraft guns also guided by radar. It was not necessary to so equip all searchlights but a system was evolved of radar-linked master searchlights that would enable other searchlights in the vicinity to join in sweeping the same or adjacent stretches of sky.

Post-war, for many years fighters were divided into day-fighters and night-fighters or all-weather fighters. Aircraft equipped with radar needed to have a two-man crew. Nevertheless, it eventually proved possible to equip single-seat aircraft with radar, while airborne radars also developed to include systems that could provide warnings of bad weather, usually detecting raindrops in cloud formations. These proved valuable in that airliners were able to navigate their way around bad weather and avoid severe turbulence that could, in extreme cases, tear an aircraft apart.

The age of the guided missile saw yet more new roles appear for radar. Many missiles, especially those used for air defence, were 'beam-riding', meaning that they followed the beam of the defending radar to the target, such as an approaching enemy aircraft. Other later missiles were fitted with their own radar which locked onto a target, even if evasive action was taken.

Radar is used not just for navigation or for offence and defence but is the basis of modern air traffic control systems, both for en route direction and for airport terminal manoeuvring zones. The ideal airport is not just one that has radar for aircraft on approach but also ground radar systems so that aircraft can be directed on the ground as well as in the air at all times of the day and night. Transponders aboard aircraft provide identification details to air traffic controllers, who can tell an aircraft's height and speed as well as its direction.

An important development in recent years has been the 'Traffic Alert and Collision Avoidance System' (TACAS), which warns aircraft of an impending collision with another aircraft or the ground and directs the pilots in the direction needed to avoid such an eventuality. The current system is improved and known as TACAS II. This helps to avoid what is known as 'Controlled Flight into Terrain' (CFIT), and which has for many years been one of the major intractables in improving airline safety.

Radar works best on metal and less well on materials such as wood or plastic. Therefore ships built of wood or glass-reinforced plastic have to hoist a metal target so that they may be 'seen'.

Less happily (for some), radar has also become the essential ingredient in police speed traps intended to catch motor vehicles exceeding a local speed limit.

Chapter 4

Electronic Warfare

In reading this book, it becomes self-evident that any development is followed by a counter-development. For example, spears, swords, bows and arrows were all countered by shields, helmets and then body armour, and even armour for horses. The warship category known as destroyers might sound aggressive but in fact they were initially defensive, having their origins in the torpedo-boat destroyer developed at the end of the nineteenth and beginning of the twentieth century to counter what was then regarded as the growing menace to the warships of the day, the torpedo-boat. The prevailing logic had it that such small, fast, cheap and lightly-manned warships fitted with torpedoes presented a massive threat to the large battle fleets of the day and had to be countered by small, fast, cheap and lightly-manned torpedo-boat destroyers.

Electronic warfare or electronic countermeasures of a basic kind date from the Russo-Japanese War of 1904–05, after the first flight of an aeroplane but pre-dating the use of aircraft in warfare. This initial application would today be regarded as radio-jamming. During the war, Russian wireless stations at Port Arthur on the coast of mainland China jammed wireless telegraphy between Japanese warships, using the spark-gap transmitters to generate noise disrupting Japanese attempts to coordinate the bombardment of the Russian naval base.

During the First World War, both the United Kingdom and Germany attempted to interfere with each other's wireless transmissions along the Western Front, while the Admiralty intercepted German naval transmissions with attempts at jamming signals and the sending of false radio transmissions.

It naturally followed that radar had to be countered. This has become a fine and varied art but it is significant that elements of the early radar-jamming techniques are still in use. The technology has since expanded to include electronic countermeasures and other means such as protective coatings and changes to the shape of ships and aircraft to provide what are known as 'stealth' features.

Not surprisingly, the first radio countermeasures, which would now be described as electronic warfare, were designed to counter the UK's Chain

Home radar network. In September 1940 the Luftwaffe established a ground station near Calais, using Breslau spot-noise jammers to neutralize the Chain Home radars. This caused some difficulties for the RAF but at no time was it serious and approaching German formations were always successfully detected.

At the same time, the RAF created its own jamming unit, No. 80 Wing, using a jammer code-named 'Aspirin' to counter the German *Knickebein*. Aspirin produced Morse dashes on the same frequencies as the German beams but not synchronized with them and this prevented *Knickebein* from achieving its full potential. When the more sophisticated *X-Gerat* navigational system appeared, a more sophisticated jammer was required, able to operate at higher frequencies; this was code-named 'Bromide'. The advent of *Y-Gerat* also required further development of jamming and the next variant was code-named 'Domino'.

This cat-and-mouse game of improving navigational and bomb-aiming systems followed by further development of jamming came to an end when the invasion of the Soviet Union by German forces, Operation BARBAROSSA, saw the Luftwaffe diverted to the Eastern Front. Nevertheless, German jammers located on the French coast played a part in the successful escape through the English Channel by the German battlecruisers *Scharnhorst* and *Gneisenau* and the cruiser *Prinz Eugen* in February 1942, despite elaborate plans having been prepared by the British to prevent these three important warships escaping to Germany.

Chaff

The most basic radar countermeasure is today known as chaff, although originally known to the British as 'window'. Just as work on pulse-emitting radars was conducted simultaneously in the UK, the USA and Germany, so too was work on chaff, known to the Germans as *Düppel* after the Berlin suburb in which it was developed. Put simply, chaff consists of strips of paper, glass fibre or plastic covered in aluminium, or even strips of aluminium itself, although this is more expensive and using paper has the added advantage that when thrown out of an aircraft, it hangs around in the air longer and prolongs the effect. The chaff then appears as a cluster of targets on a radar screen or swamps the screen with multiple returns.

As early as 1937 Gerald Touch, working with Robert Watson-Watt on the development of radar, realized that suspending lengths of wire from balloons or parachutes could overwhelm a radar system by producing false echoes. Another researcher, R.V. Jones, suggested that dropping pieces of metal foil would have the same result. This idea was taken further by Welsh scientist Joan Curran, who worked at the Telecommunications Research Establishment (TRE), and in 1942 suggested that packets of aluminium strips should be dumped to generate a cloud of false echoes. The early years of the war had seen the RAF dumping propaganda leaflets over Germany and at first it was thought that the strips should be the size of a notebook page, overprinted to act as propaganda leaflets. Nevertheless, it was soon discovered that the most effective form of chaff or window was strips of black paper backed with aluminium foil, exactly 10.63in × 0.79in (27cm × 2cm), packed into bundles each weighing 1lb (0.45kg). Head of the TRE, A.P. Rowe, chose the code name 'window'.

Realizing that the Germans had almost certainly conducted research along the same lines, there was hesitation on the part of the RAF to use window at first, for fear that the Germans would also use it and nullify the value of the Chain Home network. Even if the Germans hadn't produced a similar system, they would realize immediately that their radar systems were being jammed and once samples of window were collected after the raid, would be able to reproduce it themselves with little delay. This point was made bluntly by the British government's leading scientific adviser, Professor Frederick Lindemann, later Lord Cherwell. The fears this raised among the leaders of RAF Fighter Command and Anti-Aircraft Command of a new blitz being launched delayed the use of window until July 1943, by which time the new centimetric radar being used by the RAF was felt to be capable of dealing with any Luftwaffe use of chaff. It was also discovered by examining a captured German *Würzburg* radar and by reconnaissance that German radars were limited to three frequency ranges and so were more prone to jamming than British radar.

Approval was finally given for the use of window for Operation GOMORRAH, the fire raids against Hamburg. The first air-crews trained to use window were those of RAF Bomber Command's No. 76 Squadron. Twenty-four crews were briefed on how to drop the bundles of aluminized-paper strips, one every minute through the flare chute. One German radar operator is recorded as having wailed that the bombers 'were multiplying themselves', although this effect was also increased by having aircraft flying at different levels above one another before spreading out for the bombing. The results were spectacular. The radar-guided master searchlights wandered aimlessly across the sky while AA guns fired randomly or not at all and the night-fighters, their radar displays swamped with false echoes, utterly failed to find the bomber stream. The result was the devastation of a vast area of Hamburg with more than

40,000 civilian casualties for the loss of only twelve bombers. Squadrons soon had special chutes fitted to their bombers to make the deployment even easier.

The Germans had hesitated to use *Düppel* for the same reasons that the British had hesitated to use window. All that could be done was for ground radar operators to direct fighters to the area of the greatest concentration of chaff in the belief that this also indicated the presence of bombers. This technique was known as *Wilde Sau* (Wild Boar). The fighters then had to try to pick out the bombers highlighted against the fires burning below. When the Germans finally used *Düppel*, the size of their bomber formation was so small and the number of night-fighters put into the air by the RAF so substantial that the Luftwaffe's bombers were found despite the chaff.

In the United States, initial tests with chaff were unsuccessful as the strips of foil clumped together into a bundle but a modification solved this problem. Meanwhile, the USAAF had introduced a spot-noise jammer: the APT-2 'Carpet' which was first issued in October 1943 to counter the German *Würzburg* anti-aircraft radars. The Germans widened the range of frequencies used by their radars but in return Carpet was also modified. An audio output was also added to the radar systems so that operators could hear propeller noise through the disruption caused by chaff.

The Germans also introduced a new radar for their night-fighters during the winter of 1943–44 with a lower frequency that overcame the most serious effects of chaff. This turned the tables, most noticeably on the night of 30/31 March 1944 when 94 out of a force of 795 British bombers attacking Nuremberg were shot down. Fortunately, three months later the RAF captured a Junkers Ju 88 night-fighter complete with the new SN-2 radar and tests revealed that the radar was vulnerable to long lengths of foil known as 'rope'. By that summer, the new German airborne radar was also neutralized.

Post-war, the main application for chaff was for use by warships to distract radar-guided missiles as they approached. Most modern warships are fitted with chaff dispensers for this reason but this is very much a last-minute means of defence after other systems such as anti-missile guns and missiles have been bypassed.

Normandy

The Normandy landings that began on 6 June 1944 comprised the largest amphibious operation in history and also the most numerous airborne landings. Some 7,000 vessels of all kinds were used, apart from aircraft carriers for which there was no room and no need as the landing areas were within easy distance of the south coast of England. The landings had been long awaited, not least because the Soviet dictator Stalin constantly demanded a Second Front, ignoring the fact that in North Africa, then Italy, and also in the Pacific and Burma the British and American Allies already had other fronts. In addition, they were mounting a massive combined bombing offensive over Axis-occupied territory on a scale not matched by anything the Soviet air force was doing, were also fighting the Battle of the Atlantic, and fighting both the weather and the Germans in order to carry supplies to Russian ports north of the Arctic Circle.

Much had been done to confuse the Germans, with Hitler expecting the Allies to return to Europe via Norway, while many of his senior officers expected landings in the Pas de Calais area rather than Normandy. Nevertheless, the Allies could not depend entirely on the element of surprise and were never completely sure that the Germans had swallowed the false leads put out by the British and the Americans.

The Germans had a network of radar stations along the coast of France, as well as having sentries and lookouts posted. Ground stations in England pinpointed the position of the German radar stations and fighter-bombers were deployed on 2,000 sorties against these targets. On the night of the invasion fleet crossing the English Channel, both shipborne and airborne jamming was applied. Two squadrons of aircraft, all modified bombers, flew along the line of the River Somme jamming the German night-fighter control frequencies. This was part of a massive effort to keep the Germans grounded so that their aircraft did not spot the massive invasion fleet. The weather also played a part, as many Germans including the senior commanders on the ground believed that the conditions were too bad for an invasion and indeed, Operation OVERLORD had been delayed for twenty-four hours because of it.

There were no fewer than five beaches in Normandy chosen for the landings but two fleets were seen by the Germans to be heading for Le Havre and Boulogne. These fleets had no ships; instead, the RAF was mounting Operation TAXABLE. Avro Lancaster bombers of the RAF's crack 617 Squadron, originally formed for the famous raid on the Ruhr dams, were dropping the thin aluminium strips known as window to simulate on enemy radar an invasion force approaching Cap d'Antifer, north of Le Havre, while motor launches towed reflector balloons intended to create an image of large ships on enemy radar. A similar operation was mounted around Boulogne with Short Stirling bombers dropping window in what was known as Operation GLIMMER.

Jamming

That same year (1944), the RAF formed No. 100 Group with five squadrons of heavy bombers fitted to act as specialized jamming aircraft. These were escorted by six squadrons of de Havilland Mosquito night-fighters that were also part of the group. To enable the Mosquito crews to find German aircraft in the darkness and not to attack a friendly aircraft by mistake, a couple of different devices were fitted to the Mosquitos. One of these was 'Serrate' which homed in on the pulses from German fighter radars, while the other was 'Perfectos', transmitting pulses that interrogated the German IFF (Identification Friend or Foe) frequencies. German aircraft replied to the Perfectos transmissions and were shot down as a result.

In the Pacific the Japanese were lagging behind the Americans and British in many respects, including for example sonar, while their radar technology by 1945 was no further advanced than that of the Germans much earlier in the war. No airborne radar was in use by the end of the war and the country's radar defences were relatively crude, even though the USAAF's Boeing B-29 Superfortress heavy bombers flew very high, which also had the effect of making them difficult for Japanese fighters to reach unless they stripped out guns and ammunition and flew suicide *kamikaze* missions, as many did against the bombers.

Japan's poor level of protection had to face the latest in jamming technology from the USAAF. On daylight raids the bombers flew in close formation with each aircraft covering its neighbours with its strong gunnery defences, while massive electronic jamming was accompanied by streams of the aforementioned rope. At night, the formations were much less tight for safety reasons and while the same defences were used, a small number of B-29s were equipped as specialized jamming aircraft known as 'Porcupines', with their bomb bays carrying up to eighteen separate jamming transmitters and up to a ton of rope while the aircraft circled the target area jamming the defensive radars. The Japanese radar defences collapsed in the face of such an onslaught. A good measure of the success of the B-29 over Japan was that their loss rate was just 0.8 per cent; the lowest of any of the war's major bombing campaigns. The collapse of the Japanese air defence radar had only been matched once before in the war when the attacks on Hamburg started in July 1943 but while the Germans recovered from this setback, the Japanese did not and could not.

These techniques remained available after the war but the emphasis moved more to electronic jamming, more usually described today as electronic countermeasures. The Korean War was fought on a more primitive basis, accounted for in part by the lack of major industrial areas and significant targets. Many of the operational sorties were by fighter-bombers and their targets, while including the occasional bridge, could be as poor as an ox and cart. Vietnam was far more sophisticated but even so, the North Vietnamese often countered the USAAF's B-52 heavy bombers by firing anti-aircraft missiles in salvoes; a costly but effective means of defence until the Americans started using stand-off weapons which were more accurate as well as being safer for the attacking aircraft and its crew. The Falklands campaign of 1982 saw improvised chaff dispensers fitted to British Aerospace Sea Harriers. RAF Avro Vulcan bombers flew anti-radar missions against the Argentine-held airfield at Port Stanley.

Modern electronic countermeasures (ECM) consist of electrical or electronic devices designed to trick or deceive radar, sonar or other detection systems such as infrared or lasers. A typical system can make many separate targets appear to the enemy or make the real target appear to disappear or move about randomly. Most air forces use ECM to protect their aircraft from attack, especially from air-to-air or surface-to-air guided missiles. It is also used by warships and even on some battle tanks to fool guided missiles and is frequently coupled with stealth advances so that the ECM systems have an easier job. Offensive ECM usually means jamming, while defensive ECM still often takes the form of blip enhancement and jamming of missile homing devices.

Today, while ECM is used by most military units, aircraft remain the most important users. ECM is used to keep aircraft from being tracked by search radars or targeted by surface-to-air or air-to-air missiles. An aircraft ECM can take the form of an attachable underwing pod or can be located within the airframe. Fighter planes using a conventional electronically-scanned antenna mount dedicated jamming pods instead or, in the case of a number of air forces including those of the US, Germany and Italy, may be accompanied on their missions by dedicated ECM units.

Chapter 5

Identification Friend or Foe (IFF)

Aircraft identification is a fine art. During the Second World War identification was so bad that when the Allies prepared to invade Normandy, they painted black and white stripes on the fuselages and wings of their aircraft. In the Far East, the Royal Air Force and the Royal Navy's Fleet Air Arm abandoned their normal camouflage roundels of a red circle surrounded by a dark blue border and instead used light blue in the centre of the roundel. One Fleet Air Arm pilot flying Fairey Swordfish on anti-submarine patrols covering the Arctic convoys soon discovered to his discomfort that the anti-aircraft gunners on the ships of the convoy could not tell the difference between his single-engine biplane and the German Junkers Ju 88, a sleek twin-engine monoplane!

In an air war that could be fought in the dark or in poor visibility, the ability to distinguish between friend and foe was as important as ever but much more difficult. Aircraft began to be fitted with devices that enabled them to show to the radar defences that they were friendly. The devices fitted to British aircraft produced an echo on a radar screen that appeared as a distinctive elongated blip. This device was switched on when the aircraft was about 40 miles from the British coast. Unfortunately, at first many pilots believed that the device would also jam German radar when in fact it enabled German night-fighters to home in on the British bombers.

Chapter 6

Combined Operations

Combined operations or 'Combined Ops' could clearly be argued to have preceded the Second World War by many centuries. After all, armies needing to move by sea needed ships for their amphibious landings, for re-supply and for withdrawal if all did not go well. To the British, combined operations were virtually synonymous with amphibious warfare but by the Second World War, amphibious warfare without strong air support was unthinkable.

Amphibious warfare was brought to an advanced stage of sophistication during the Second World War but many lessons had to be learned first. The Japanese have generally been regarded as the earliest exponents but in Europe it dates from before the Battle of Marathon in 490 BC.

Nevertheless, there are also records that suggest much earlier attempts at invasion from the sea using what might be described as 'light forces', i.e. without cavalry, especially by the so-called 'Sea Peoples', originally Phoenicians, who migrated in substantial numbers around the shores of the Mediterranean, colonizing Cyprus and Malta. Amidst these rare attempts at amphibious assault there were many more migrations and Doric Sparta and Ionian Athens established colonies or trading posts around the Eastern Mediterranean. Eventually these movements resulted in rivalry leading to war.

In 490 BC during the Second Persian Campaign came what was generally regarded as the first amphibious assault, at least in the West, because the ships were specially constructed to carry horses and cavalry, with the Persian troops being carried direct to Attica, the region to the west of Athens, pausing only to take Rhodes and Naxos on their way. These forces landed near Marathon, only to find their way blocked by the Greeks. Rather than attack, the Persians re-embarked, putting their cavalry aboard first; a mistake as the Greeks then attacked the Persian force in strength. Later, in the Third Persian Campaign, a novel feature was the construction of two bridges across a chain of boats to keep open the route across the Hellespont.

Clearly, even before the Romans, amphibious assault was not unknown and indeed, in the ability to land cavalry or to improvise bridges using boats there was a degree of sophistication. Records of the numbers involved are few but when the Athenian trading post at Segesta in Sicily called for assistance, being threatened by Syracuse which was an ally of Corinth at the time (415–413 BC), the Athenians sent 134 triremes with 25,000 men in their ships' companies and 6,400 soldiers.

The Greeks and the Phoenicians were the great seafaring powers of the ancient world, even to the extent that the Persians had to depend on conscripted Phoenician sailors and ships to make progress across the Eastern Mediterranean. Early Rome was not a sea power and it was not until later that Rome began to appreciate its value and started to confront the growing power of Carthage in the Punic Wars. The catalyst for this was the need to secure Sicily as part of the Roman Empire. Initially the battles for Sicily were on land but the need for a fleet soon became obvious and the Romans chose a stranded Punic quinquereme or *pentere* as the model for the ships of the fleet. An innovation was the boarding ramp known as the *corvus* (meaning 'raven'), enabling enemy ships to be seized by boarding parties of soldiers. Despite their inexperience in sea warfare, the new fleet enabled the Romans to seize Corsica in 259 BC and then Malta in 257 BC.

During the Napoleonic Wars, the threat of a French invasion of England was real. There were few innovations but a print from the period showed massive *montgolfières*, or hot air balloons, each carrying up to 3,000 French troops, horses and cannon across the English Channel. This startling prophecy of what would have been an airborne assault with air-landed forces remained a dream. The technology of the early balloons was simply not up to what was required and in any case, the unpredictability of the wind over the Channel would have made the operation hazardous. Nevertheless, the concept of an assault using air power could fairly be said to have dated from this time.

Perhaps more of a foretaste of what would unfold in the twentieth century came with the Walcheren expedition of August 1809, when the Royal Navy landed what was for the time the considerable force of 40,000 men on the island of Walcheren using 520 transports escorted by 42 ships of the line (predecessors of the battleship), 25 frigates and 60 smaller vessels under the overall command of Rear Admiral Strachan. The Dutch port of Vlissingen was captured but an assault on Antwerp failed and the troops suffered heavy losses before being re-embarked.

For the British, the term 'combined operations' was synonymous with amphibious warfare; something that was not new to such a leading maritime power. Yet for centuries there was no overall command or co-ordination of naval and land forces.

During the First World War there was the notorious invasion of Gallipoli for the land war, also known as the Dardanelles for the maritime element, and which was from the outset a major amphibious operation. Yet few now realize that there was a plan for an even more audacious amphibious operation that would have meant nothing less than the sea-borne invasion of Germany itself, with landings on the Baltic coast of Pomerania, the closest point to the capital, just 80 miles from Berlin. This aborted plan and the Gallipoli landings had one thing in common: both were attempts to break the stalemate on the Western Front that saw little substantial movement until mid-1918 and bring an early end to the war that at first many had predicted would be 'all over by Christmas'.

So what distinguished the Second World War from the First World War and indeed earlier conflicts, when armies needed navies to fulfil their strategic aims? What gave combined operations a worthwhile edge during the Second World War was air power. Air power had eventually been deployed over Gallipoli but not when it was most needed, at the outset. When the commander of the operation, General Sir Ian Hamilton, and his chief of staff Major General Walter Braithwaite, met Kitchener to discuss the operation for the first time, Braithwaite proposed that the invasion force should have better air power than the enemy and aired the possibility of having a squadron of the latest aircraft manned by experienced pilots and observers. Kitchener turned on him, his face red with fury, and barked: 'Not one!'

The war in the air was already making an impact on the Western Front by this time and Kitchener's refusal to recognize its potential over Gallipoli cannot easily be explained. In fact, the Royal Naval Air Service (RNAS) did operate reconnaissance missions over Gallipoli and the Dardanelles – even taking up at least one submarine commander to give him a good idea of the situation – and conducted some bombing missions but the quantity of bombs made available was rationed and completely inadequate.

Collaboration between the land forces and those at sea was poor, with the Royal Navy supposed to move landing stages to the shores of Gallipoli but instead subcontracting the duty to ship owners so that only one of twelve was actually delivered. The sequence of events leading up to the invasion saw the Royal Navy effectively alert the Turks and the Germans to the importance of the peninsula. In this instance, the sole success for navy-army cooperation was the British withdrawal.

Combined Operations in the Second World War

From the start of hostilities during the Second World War, air power was the vital ingredient missing from earlier conflicts and deployed on a scale not seen during the First World War. Not only the aeroplane but also air forces had matured into effective fighting machines. Another vital ingredient was inter-service collaboration on an unprecedented scale.

One major step forward was the establishment of the Inter-Services Training and Development Centre (ISTDC) in May 1938. The initial work was two-pronged, dealing with the problems of landing on a defended beach while also looking at developing landing craft, with prototypes being built.

Much of the credit for the importance and eventual success of combined operations goes to Britain's wartime prime minister, Winston Churchill, who from the start pressed for combined operations. While these were to culminate in the series of major invasions across the Mediterranean that preceded the Normandy landings in June 1944, even as British forces were withdrawing from Dunkirk, Churchill decided on a policy of raids on enemy-occupied territory. Churchill had his attention drawn to a certain young naval officer and in 1941 appointed Lord Louis Mountbatten as Chief Advisor of Combined Operations with the rank of acting commodore in October 1941. Promotion to vice-admiral followed in April 1942 and the equivalent rank in the other two services: that is lieutenant-general in the army and air marshal in the Royal Air Force. Aged just 42 at the time, Mountbatten also became a de facto member of the British Chiefs of Staff Committee.

Churchill was impatient for offensive action. Mountbatten had established a reputation for daring and was a colourful character but he had been conspicuously unsuccessful as the commander of a destroyer flotilla. Noel Coward's film *In Which We Serve* did much to publicize his exploits and, with a strong propaganda message, undoubtedly put a gloss on his efforts. That may have been well for the public and members of the armed forces but perhaps it also influenced Churchill. While the raids on Bruneval and St Nazaire had been planned before he took up his post, he was responsible for them. The Dieppe raid had been postponed due to bad weather and the officer who had been most closely involved, the then General Bernard Montgomery, wanted it to be cancelled but was transferred to North Africa to take command of the British Eighth Army.

After many delays the Dieppe raid, Operation JUBILEE, took place on 19 August 1942 but the cover was blown completely. Security was non-existent; so too was intelligence about enemy strength and dispositions and the terrain. Most of the troops involved were Canadian as their commanders were keen for their men to see action but they were assisted by Royal Marine Commandos, the Royal Navy and the Royal Air Force. Starting at 0450hrs, withdrawal began at 1100hrs under heavy fire and took until 1400hrs. When it left, the assault force left behind 3,367 Canadians who had been killed, wounded or taken prisoner, as well as 275 RM commandos. The Royal Navy lost a destroyer and 33 landing craft, with 550 men killed or wounded. The RAF lost 106 aircraft. By comparison, the Germans lost just 591 men killed or wounded and 48 aircraft.

Before this, Mountbatten's predecessor, Admiral of the Fleet Sir Roger Keyes who had been brought back out of retirement after the fall of France and whose First World War record had included the successful Zeebrugge raid, had established a Combined Operations Headquarters in London, removing his personnel from the Admiralty. This, and the establishment of a training centre at Inveraray in Scotland followed by others in Egypt and India, was meant to indicate the independence of combined operations from the control of any single arm of the British armed forces. When Mountbatten took over, he had nine senior American officers seconded to COHQ, establishing the first international tri-service organization of its kind.

COHQ developed into not only being tri-service and international but also a centre for experiment, design and development of the craft and other equipment needed to make combined operations really work.

The success of the landings on Madagascar, Operation IRONCLAD, in March 1942 to prevent this Vichy French territory from being used by the Axis powers was little preparation for an assault on a heavily-defended area, as was to be the case at Dieppe. It was the debacle at Dieppe that was the driving force behind the development of specialized landing craft.

COHQ grew to 350 personnel by April 1943, while it controlled 89 landing ships logistics (LSL), more than 2,600 landing craft and 50,000 men. This led to the command being decentralized and Mountbatten's naval responsibilities being handed back to the Admiralty. Nevertheless, a new headquarters was established ready for the Normandy landings, again with British and American officers and with many former COHQ personnel involved.

Mountbatten's successor, Major General Robert Laycock, reported to the British chiefs of staff but was not one of them, although he usually attended their meetings and had access to Churchill. Laycock controlled the commandos, which included units of the British army as well as of the Royal Marines, an integral part of the Royal Navy. He was responsible for small-scale raids but not for major assaults, although those commanding such operations were obliged to seek his advice.

To a great extent, combined operations were encouraged by the appointment of commanders-in-chief in the various theatres of war who brought together the subordinate air, land and sea commanders.

A good example of how this worked came with the Normandy landings, led by the Supreme Allied Commander, General of the Army Dwight D. Eisenhower. Air Chief Marshal (equivalent to a USAAF four-star general) Sir Arthur Tedder was Eisenhower's deputy, while the British General Sir Bernard Montgomery was appointed commander of the Allied ground forces and Admiral Sir Bertram Ramsay commanded the naval aspects of the landings.

Not only were troops landed from the air and from the sea (the latter being by far the stronger force) with a heavy bombardment by mainly British warships but also those from the United States navy and the 'Free' navies of occupied nations plus bombing by the Royal Air Force and United States Army Air Force, but the Royal Navy and RAF Coastal Command ensured that German naval units could not attack the invasion force. Before the landings, 'Combined Operations Pilotage Parties' (COPPs) reconnoitred the beaches, mines were cleared ahead of the invasion fleet and obstacles and mines were removed from the beaches as the first landing craft swept ashore, aided, on the approach to the British beaches, by midget submarines sitting on the surface and shining lights to seaward so that the landings occurred in exactly the right places.

The mistakes of Dieppe were not repeated and the lessons learned during the landings in North Africa, Sicily and Italy were all used. The sole exception at Normandy was that there were no aircraft carriers: in the confined spaces of the English Channel, already packed with the largest invasion fleet ever known, there was no room for them and with air bases as close as 80 miles away, no need either. Shore-based naval aircraft helped to patrol the waters on either side of the invasion fleet, looking mainly for German submarines, U-boats and fast attack vessels known as E-boats.

Lessons had been learned elsewhere as well. In North Africa, the Desert Air Force brought air-ground coordination to a stage that had not been reached before and this aided the advance through Italy. By the time of the Normandy landings, the Allies had two tactical air forces – one predominantly American and the other predominantly of the UK and British Empire – that accompanied the ground forces as they advanced towards

Germany and that eventually had bases in Germany itself as the war drew to a close.

Post-war, not only had the lesson that the democracies had to work together, unite and exercise their armed forces together been taken on board but it was also clear that close cooperation between different services had to be standard practice. However, this did not mean ending the distinctions between the different services. In many countries, including the United Kingdom, army air corps were established with armies having their own air power once again, while in the United States an autonomous United States Air Force was established and the US army also established its own air corps suitable for liaison and battlefield transport and attack. Nevertheless, closer liaison and training in joint operations remained important.

The new regime stood the test of the Korean War and in many ways was successful during the Anglo-French landings in the Suez Canal Zone in 1956. Yet this operation, known as MUSKETEER, is seldom referred to in British naval and military history as it was a tactical success but a political failure.

To some extent, combined operations have been helped by the ending of duplication in military capability. In the United States, the practice of each service having its own air transport capability ended with the creation of the USAF-controlled Military Air Transport Service, while maritime-reconnaissance was no longer provided by the USAAF and the US navy but entirely by the latter service. In the United Kingdom, heavy-lift helicopters became the preserve of the Royal Air Force, although naval medium-lift helicopters catered for the Royal Marines.

Separate service ministries have now disappeared in most countries in favour of a unified defence ministry, as in the case of the US Pentagon and the British Ministry of Defence.

Chapter 7

Special Forces

What would today be recognized as special forces pre-dated the Second World War by several centuries but the activity can be regarded as formally dating from that conflict with the creation of specially-trained units that have in turn pre-dated elite units such as the British army's Special Air Service (SAS) and the Special Boat Service (SBS) of the Royal Marines.

The term 'special forces' covers those who are able to conduct reconnaissance and surveillance on the ground in a hostile environment, such as beach reconnaissance before an invasion; support counter-insurgency operations or, on the other hand, conduct or support counter-terrorism operations; sabotage and demolition, other than that conducted by terrorist or resistance movements; hostage rescue; and training and development of the security forces of a friendly state.

China and Japan had the forerunners of today's special forces, used to seize commanding heights before a battle, conduct reconnaissance, sabotage and assassinations. The Romans used fast ships camouflaged and manned by specially-selected crews for scouting and commando missions, as indeed did the Muslims later during the crusades with crews who could pass as crusaders and fool enemy ships into coming close enough to be boarded and captured. During the Napoleonic Wars, special sniper and sapper units were formed to operate independently from the main battle units.

In the nineteenth century, the British Indian army had two special units, the first of which was the Corps of Guides formed in 1846 to help control the border regions and especially the border with Afghanistan and which was later joined by the Gurkha Scouts during the 1890s. The experience thus gained was applied during the Second Boer War (1899–1902) when the Lovat Scouts were formed and after the Boer War became the British army's first sniper unit. While there were no formal special forces units in the First World War, troops were used on reconnaissance and kill-or-capture missions to gain knowledge of likely enemy movements. The Royal Navy, meanwhile, conducted successful raids on the German-held ports of Ostend and Zeebrugge.

The Second World War

Following the First World War, the Madden Committee called for the Royal Marines to be developed into a force for special operations and also to protect naval bases, especially those abroad. These recommendations were ignored until after the outbreak of the Second World War. With the fall of France, the new British Prime Minister Winston Churchill called for special operations and raids on enemy-held territory. In contrast to today, the commando units formed at Churchill's behest were created from both Royal Marine and British army units.

By late 1940 more than 2,000 men had volunteered and new units were formed as part of a Special Service Brigade commanded by Brigadier Charles Haydon. A dozen commandos were formed, each of around 450 men divided into 75-man troops that were in turn subdivided into 15-man sections. Commanding officers for each of the twelve commandos were lieutenant colonels. In December of that year, a Middle East Commando Depot was formed to train and support commando units in the Middle East and North Africa. Even so, it was not until February 1942 that a Commando Training Depot was formed at Auchnacarry in the Scottish Highlands, with hand-picked instructors providing training that was far more demanding than that expected elsewhere in the British army.

No time was wasted with the new recruits. On arrival at the nearest railway station, Spean Bridge, they had to march, carrying their equipment, the 8 miles to the commando depot. Exercises used live ammunition and explosives so that training was as realistic as possible. Marches to test speed and endurance were routed across the Highlands and over assault courses, carrying arms and full equipment by day and by night. Apart from training on a wide range of weapons, there was also unarmed combat, small boat operations and map-reading.

The result was that peak wartime strength of more than thirty units was eventually reached and these served in all theatres of war. Usually operating in small groups, for the major assaults in Europe and Asia operations were at brigade strength. These units formed the basis of the Parachute Regiment, the SAS and the SBS, as for much of the Second World War standard infantry regiments were allocated to parachute operations.

The SAS itself originated from an idea of Lieutenant David Stirling who had volunteered in June 1940 for No. 8 Commando, later known as 'Layforce'. When Layforce was disbanded, Stirling had the idea that a small force of highly-trained soldiers with the advantage of surprise could inflict damage on the enemy out of all proportion to their numbers. He believed that small teams of paratroops could operate behind enemy lines, obtaining intelligence, destroying equipment including aircraft and attacking supply lines. After a meeting with the Commander-in-Chief Middle East, General Sir Claude Auchinleck, his plan was supported. Brigadier Dudley Clarke, in charge of deception in the Middle East and North Africa, had created a fictitious unit, 1st Special Air Service Brigade, to convince the Germans that the British had a significant airborne unit based in Egypt and Stirling's new unit, officially No. 2 Troop of Middle East Commando, was soon attached to the 1st Special Air Service Brigade as 'L Detachment' in October 1941.

Stirling's force often operated in conjunction with the Long Range Desert Group (LRDG) that had been formed in Egypt in June 1940 as the Long Range Patrol by Major Ralph Bagnold and dated from the time of General Archibald Wavell as C-in-C Middle East. The LRDG consisted of volunteers and its strength never exceeded 350 men. Nevertheless, its impact was considerable and in addition to obtaining intelligence and conducting raids on enemy positions, the LRDG was often used to guide other formations because of its expertise in desert navigation.

Operating together, the two organizations enjoyed many successes, with one of Stirling's men, Paddy Mayne, destroying 47 enemy aircraft in a single night, which was on a par with the RAF's highest-scoring fighter ace, Pat Prattle, who was credited with between 40 and 50 enemy aircraft. In November 1942, Stirling's force became 1st SAS Regiment.

The Special Boat Service can trace its origins to a British unit formed in July 1940 by Roger Courtney, a commando officer. As with its shore-based counterparts, reconnaissance and sabotage were its primary roles. Known initially as the Folboat Troop after the folding canoes used on raids, the unit then became the Special Boat Section. From April 1941 it worked with Layforce and was responsible for several successful operations in the Mediterranean and then briefly became part of Middle East Commando. This unit was renamed 1st SBS and attached to the Special Air Service as its D Squadron in December 1941 after Courtney returned to the UK to form 2nd SBS. In April 1943 the SAS was disbanded and its D Squadron was re-formed as the Special Boat Squadron. Over the next fifteen months it operated in the Aegean and conducted 381 raids. Meanwhile, 2nd SBS took Major General Mark Clark ashore before the start of the North African landings, Operation TORCH, in November 1942. It later undertook the beach reconnaissance for the Salerno landings, Operation AVALANCHE, before moving to Ceylon for operations in the Far East.

Naturally, the Allies did not have a monopoly on special forces. The invasion of Belgium and The Netherlands started with glider-landed special forces taking the fort of Eben-Emael, imprisoning the occupants and enabling the German armies to cross the Rhine. Some time later, *Hauptsturmführer* Otto Skorzeny led the German 502nd SS *Jäger* Battalion, which conducted raids behind Allied lines. Its most daring operation was the rescue of the deposed Italian dictator, Benito Mussolini, from imprisonment in a hotel on the Grand Sasso, part of the Abruzzi range. This was 9,000 feet high and could only be reached by a funicular railway, which had been closed. On 12 September 1943, twelve DFS230 gliders were towed by Heinkel He 126s from Rome, landing successfully on a ledge by the hotel despite poor weather. Mussolini's guards were taken by surprise and surrendered, allowing Mussolini to be freed by the Germans. A small Fieseler Storch army liaison aeroplane landed and, despite Skorzeny insisting on joining Mussolini and the pilot, succeeded in taking off and carrying Mussolini to Rome where he was installed as a German puppet ruler.

For the D-Day Normandy landings, while the formal reconnaissance was provided for the British army by the Royal Navy and Royal Air Force, there was also help from the French resistance, aided and armed by the British Special Operations Executive (SOE) and the American Office of Strategic Services (OSS). The French resistance was a substantial organization and in May 1944 its strength has been estimated at 100,000 personnel ready to take orders from General Koenig, head of the Free French Forces of the Interior, as well as between 35,000 and 45,000 *maquis* (French guerrilla forces) who were armed, although many only had sufficient ammunition to fight for a day. The mainstay of the resistance's work was sabotage, frequently disrupting the railway system and communications.

There were other forms of resistance and sabotage. One of these was the 'Cooney' teams comprising eighteen units, each of three French Special Air Servicemen, all uniformed, who were parachuted into Brittany on the night of 7/8 June 1944 to cut railway links with Normandy, thereby preventing the German 3rd Parachute Division being moved to Normandy by train.

Teams of three seemed to be the ideal, as this was also the basis of the 'Jedburgh' teams, unusual in that they were all in uniform, each consisting of an Englishman, an American and a Frenchman. These were first dropped into France at the time of the Normandy landings but follow-up teams were also dropped in France for the next ten weeks.

The members of the Jedburgh teams were drawn from the SOE and the OSS. Their role was to coordinate the work of the French resistance and the *maquis*, ensure that they worked towards fulfilling the Allied aims and also act as a 'staff' for the resistance groups. This was important as there was considerable rivalry between resistance groups with differing political outlooks. The teams were kept supplied with arms and each included two officers and a sergeant wireless operator. Each member was trained in guerrilla warfare and sabotage. A total of 93 teams were dropped and of the 279 personnel involved, 21 were killed.

A third element in gathering intelligence was the Sussex teams, each of two men and run by the *Bureau Central de Renseignements et d'Action*, OSS and the British MI6. Members were recruited from French forces who switched to the Allies after the invasion of North Africa and all were trained by MI6. They transmitted information about German movements around the time of the Normandy landings, with the first team dropped in February 1944 and by the end of May there were thirteen of them. In contrast to the Cooney and Jedburgh teams, the members of the Sussex teams did not wear uniform.

The British special forces influenced the creation of similar forces in other Allied countries, including Australia and New Zealand, that had contributed men to the British forces. The most significant of the other forces raised was the United States army's Rangers or 'Green Berets'. Given this background, it is all the more surprising that after the Second World War ended, the British government saw no further need for the force and disbanded it on 8 October 1945. However, there was a change of heart the following year and it was decided that a new SAS regiment should be raised but as part of the Territorial Army, the British army's reserves. Initially the Artists Rifles, it became the new 21st SAS Regiment (V) on 1 January 1947.

It was not until 1950 that a new 21 SAS squadron was formed to fight in the Korean War; after training there was another change of heart and it was decided that the unit was not needed in Korea but instead could fight in the Malayan Emergency, where British forces were countering an insurgency by communist guerrillas. It arrived in Malaya and came under the command of Brigadier Mike Calvert who was building up a new unit known as the Malayan Scouts, SAS, which became 'A' Squadron, while 21 SAS became 'B' Squadron. They were later joined by 'C' Squadron, formed initially of Rhodesian volunteers who were later replaced by New Zealand volunteers.

In 1952 the need for a regular SAS regiment was recognized and 22 SAS Regiment was formally established. A third regiment was formed in 1959 comprising 23 SAS Regiment, with its personnel taken from the Reserve Reconnaissance Unit.

Based at Hereford since 1960, today the SAS forms part of the United Kingdom Special Forces (UKSF), which also includes the Special Boat Service (SBS), Special Reconnaissance Regiment (SRR), Special Forces Support Group (SFSG), 18 (UKSF) Signal Regiment and the Joint Special Forces Aviation Wing. In peacetime its operations consist mainly of counter-terrorism but during wartime, reconnaissance, sabotage and rescue become major roles. The director of UKSF has in recent years been upgraded from the one-star rank of brigadier to the two-star rank of major general.

UK special forces have been deployed in many operational areas including Northern Ireland, Iraq and Afghanistan. One of their rare public appearances was in ending a siege at the Iranian Embassy in London in 1980, rescuing hostages.

During the Second World War the United States created the Office of Strategic Services (OSS), which became the predecessor of the Central Intelligence Agency (CIA) and had responsibility for intelligence as well as special forces missions, with the latter now handled by the CIA's Special Activities Division. In February 1942 in the Pacific, Admiral Chester Nimitz called for raiders and the outcome was that the US Marine Corps established a battalion to secure beachheads and undertake special missions; this became known as the Marine Raiders. Later that year, Major General Lucian Truscott of the US army who was a liaison officer with the British General Staff proposed to General George Marshall that the US army should have units similar to the British Commandos and this led directly to the formation of the United States Army Rangers.

The United States navy's Sea, Land, Air teams, more usually known today as the Navy SEALs, can also trace their origins to the Second World War. Recognizing the need for reconnaissance of landing beaches, an Amphibious Scout and Raider School was formed in 1942 at Fort Pierce in Florida, with a 'Scouts and Raiders' unit formed in September from personnel drawn from the joint USN-USMC-US Army Observer Group. A Naval Special Warfare Center (NSWC) was commissioned in November 1942. Later additions included a further group of Scouts and Raiders code-named Special Service Unit No. 1 but after several successful missions in the Pacific theatre, conflicts over operational matters led to this being broken up and the naval personnel involved formed a new unit, the 7th Amphibious Scouts. Other special units included the Naval Combat Demolition Units, which saw service in the Far East and in Europe.

Post-war the US Army Rangers and the US Navy SEALs have been operational in most major conflicts including the Vietnam War, the liberation of Kuwait and the invasions of Afghanistan and Iraq. The most famous SEALs episode was the assassination of the world's most wanted man, the terrorist leader Osama bin Laden who had orchestrated the attack by hijacked airliners on the twin towers of the World Trade Center in New York and on the Pentagon in Washington on 11 September 2001. Bin Laden was killed on 1 May 2011, by Navy SEALs attacking and entering his hideout at Abbottabad, Pakistan.

One technique used by special forces in some post-war conflicts was to coordinate the activities of local guerrilla groups with air power. Typically the guerrillas would force enemy units to move by attacking them and so exposing them to aerial assault.

Special Forces Today
Few governments today deny the value of special forces, with the recognition that certain military objectives can be better attained by small teams of specialists rather than by deploying larger conventional forces. This is not to suggest that conventional forces are no longer necessary and indeed, the size and professionalism of such forces has a direct bearing on the ability to recruit and train, let alone deploy, special forces.

While most attention is centred on the British and American special forces, one of the best-trained units of the Armed Forces of the Russian Federation is the Spetsnaz GRU, the Russian army special forces. They are regarded as being among the best in the world, due to exceptionally harsh training.

One feature that most of these special forces have in common today is that little is ever said about their operations and their members are anonymous.

Chapter 8

Bomb Disposal

The idea of disposing of enemy bombs that had failed to explode or land-mines that had a timing device for a delayed explosion became prominent during the Second World War but the history goes back to the late nineteenth century. Just as today the main need for such measures arises from terrorism, so too was the problem that highlighted the need for efficient countermeasures against bombs in the late nineteenth century.

On 2 October 1874, a barge on the Regent's Canal in London carrying six barrels of petrol and 5 tons of gunpowder blew up, killing the crew and destroying a bridge, as well as cages at London Zoo which was nearby. A major in the British army's Royal Artillery was sent to investigate. The act of sabotage was the work of the Fenians, an Irish terrorist group agitating for independence for what is now the Irish Republic.

The officer sent to investigate was Sir Vivian Majendie, who was later responsible for the first modern legislation to control explosives and forming the first civilian bomb disposal teams. He also worked on bomb disposal techniques, including remote methods for handling explosives. In a further Fenian attack on London's major railway terminus at Victoria on 26 February 1884, he defused a bomb with a clockwork mechanism.

Terrorism was also behind the formation of New York's first police bomb squad in 1903. Nicknamed 'the Italian Squad', it was mainly occupied in dealing with dynamite bombs used by the Mafia to intimidate Italian immigrants.

Bomb disposal became a primarily military activity during the First World War; not just because of enemy action but because the massive expansion in munitions production and the use of inexperienced labour meant that many of the shells and bombs fired by both sides were 'duds'. The British Royal Army Ordnance Corps (RAOC) was assigned to tackle the problem. Late in the war, the Germans developed delayed-action fuses which would later lead to the production of delayed-action bombs, used extensively during the Second World War.

At this early stage, there was little basic knowledge, training or specialized tools. As soon as the means of countering one type of munitions was mastered, the enemy would change the structure, adding parts or changing them. This concept of constantly changing the way in which bombs are assembled continues to this day.

When the First World War ended, many casualties were suffered by officers in the RAOC as they attempted to make safe the many mines that had been scattered across the Western Front to hinder a surprise attack by enemy forces.

Despite the work put into bomb disposal and what would today be regarded as ordnance disposal on the Western Front, it was the Second World War that proved to be the defining moment for bomb disposal, when its modern concept emerged. Not only were the towns and cities of the United Kingdom exposed to heavy bombing by the Luftwaffe using bombs and land-mines with the latter dropped by parachute but bombs were fitted with delayed-action fuses and anti-handling devices to make disposal even more difficult and dangerous. An oddity was that while bombs were defused by members of the RAOC, the parachute-dropped land-mines were handled by members of the Royal Navy.

The growing body of British experience in this field was not overlooked by the United States army which sent observers and with British assistance a bomb disposal school was established in the United States under the US army's Ordnance Corps. Before this, in May 1941, a Naval Mine Disposal School was established at Washington, DC.

Post-war, bomb disposal teams remained in use, often having to defuse bombs discovered when clearing bomb sites for rebuilding or when mines were washed ashore or caught in trawler fishing nets. Not all of the bombs discovered were in the British Isles and one of the most challenging was the disposal of a 4,000lb 'Cookie', a British bomb dropped by the Royal Air Force over Germany during the war.

The next big challenge came when terrorist activity reappeared in Northern Ireland with the Provisional Irish Republican Army starting to use roadside bombs. Bombs used by the IRA and the Provisional IRA ranged from simple pipes filled with explosive and often with lead shot or scrap metal to enhance the damage that could be inflicted to more sophisticated devices with timers or victim-triggers and infrared triggers. These two republican groups also used mortars. Some protection to the bomb disposal, or in military terms, ordnance disposal officers, came with the use of remote-controlled devices to counter the threat, moving explosives away from where they presented a threat and then destroying them with an explosive charge. Nevertheless, over a thirty-eight-year campaign, no fewer than twenty-three ordnance disposal officers were killed.

By 1993 the RAOC had become part of the Royal Logistic Corps (RLC), following the union of five British army corps.

Prior to the invasion of Iraq in 2003, the US requested the assistance of British bomb disposal experts to make the oilfields safe from their planned sabotage by the Iraqis. These were the first British troops to enter the country, starting work before the actual invasion began.

Operations against the Taliban in Afghanistan also meant dealing with roadside bombs or improvised explosive devices (IEDs). Again, remote-controlled equipment was used but even so, bomb disposal continued to be a hazardous occupation, even by military standards. Little information is revealed about either the bombs themselves or the methods used to disarm them for fear of encouraging the enemy or providing information to other possible future dissident groups.

SECTION TWO

IN THE AIR

Overview

The First World War was not the first conflict to see the use of air power. Balloons were used for observation as far back as the Siege of Maubeuge in 1794 and during the American Civil War, as well as by the British army in expeditions in southern Africa. Even the use of the aeroplane in warfare pre-dates the First World War as aircraft were used by the Italians during the Balkan Wars. The First World War did see the evolution of the bomber and the fighter, as well as maritime-reconnaissance flying boats. It took the Second World War for massed air-raids to occur but this was simply a matter of scale.

So what were the real innovations in air power during the Second World War?

The most significant changes were the use of rockets and stand-off weapons so that air power could be exercised at a distance. In the V1 we see the prospect of cruise missiles, far more accurate than the random targeting of the V1. The V2 paved the way not only for the ballistic missile but also for space exploration. The glider bombs first used by the Germans at Salerno were the first 'stand-off weapons' as such.

Both the fighter and the bomber progressed and developed. The fighter became the interceptor, with fast-climbing aircraft able to intercept enemy aircraft, be they bombers or reconnaissance aircraft. Bombing became more accurate with the concept of interdiction bombing, as used against Amiens gaol and also against Gestapo headquarters in The Netherlands and Norway.

As aircraft speeds increased, the limitations of the propeller aircraft became clear but it might have been the pressures of war that persuaded the Luftwaffe and the RAF to consider jet-powered aircraft, revolutionizing aviation. As speeds rose, another problem occurred: that of enabling the pilot to escape from his aircraft if necessary. So the ejection seat was created.

While the use of aircraft for transport purposes dated from the First World War and in its immediate aftermath bomber-transports were used by the Royal Air Force for policing and air control in Mesopotamia, the concept became increasingly important during the Second World War, to the extent that the Royal Air Force added a Transport Command to its command structure. Air transport proved its worth in the Burma campaign, of course in the German invasion of Norway, then The Netherlands, and in the Allied landings in Sicily and in Normandy, as well as the Arnhem raid and the costly re-supply operation that followed when the expected relief of the air-landed troops by advancing ground forces was delayed.

Yet at the outset of the war, few could have foreseen that even heavy equipment such as tanks, admittedly light tanks, and artillery could be carried by air but the giant Hamilcar glider and the even larger well-named Messerschmitt *Gigant* transport showed the way. Post-war, aircraft car ferries and air freight proved to be a rapidly-growing business and it was air transport that kept Berlin re-supplied when the USSR closed off all surface access to the city.

A feature of much modern military aviation is that of in-flight refuelling. This was developed in the late 1930s to allow the Short Empire flying boats to extend their range but does not appear to have been used during the Second World War. Originally developed for the colonial and dominion routes of Imperial Airways, the Empire flying boat had a relatively short range, largely because of the easy availability of suitable refuelling stops. However, this became a marked disadvantage when Imperial Airways started transatlantic services with Pan American World Airways who possessed the longer-range Boeing 314.

Chapter 9

The Cruise Missile

Although there was earlier work between the two world wars in both the United Kingdom and the USSR on longer-range unmanned missiles, the cruise missile as we know it today really traces its origins back to the German V1 missiles of the Second World War. The V1 was one of Hitler's so-called *Vergeltungswaffen* or 'reprisal weapons', officially designated the FZG-76. The V1 was often referred to as a flying bomb or, because of the sound made by its simple pulse-jet engine, the 'buzz bomb' or 'doodle-bug'. It could carry a warhead of 1,870lb over a range of 150 miles at 400 mph.

Developed at Peenemünde on the Baltic, the V1 was engineered by a team working under Dr Wernher von Braun and was first flown in December 1942. The missile lacked any guidance system, with the course being determined before it took off along its launching ramp and then maintained by a gyroscopic stabilizer. Some later versions were air-launched, especially after the Allies overran the launch sites. The V1 was first used against London with a pre-dawn launch on 13 June 1944.

Weaknesses of the V1 were the lack of guidance, so while the missile could be aimed in the general direction of London, where it actually came down was due to wind conditions and its fuel running out, and its relatively low speed. Of 2,452 launched against London and the south-east of England, about a third either crashed or were shot down by fighter aircraft or anti-aircraft fire. Around 800 actually crashed on London, with the most serious damage and loss of life occurring on 18 June 1944 when one landed on the Guards Chapel at Wellington Barracks during a service, killing 121 people of whom 63 were soldiers.

The air-launched variant was carried by Heinkel He 111 bombers of the 3rd Group of *Kampfgeschwader* 3 and launched against Southampton and Gloucester as well as London. Up to half the air-launched weapons crashed soon after release and the accuracy of those that managed to stay in the air was less than that of the ground-launched missiles. Despite this, in autumn 1944 the air-launched force was expanded to a full *Geschwader*, *Kampfgeschwader* 53, with around 100 aircraft but by this time the Germans were running short of fuel so that operations were suspended in January

1945. In the meantime, targets in Normandy and Belgium and especially the port of Antwerp were also attacked by V1s.

A longer-range variant fired from launch sites in The Netherlands resumed attacks against London in March 1945, with 275 missiles being fired from 3 March until the end of the month.

In all, more than 10,000 V1s were launched against targets in England, of which 7,488 actually crossed the coast and 3,957 were shot down, while 3,531 reached their target areas with 2,419 reaching London, around 30 reaching Southampton and Portsmouth and 1 reaching Manchester. Deaths totalled 6,184, while a further 17,981 people were injured.

It was suggested at one stage that a manned version of the missile be developed but this was ruled out by the German high command.

The Japanese also produced a manned rocket-powered *Kamikaze* flying bomb that could be launched from a bomber but this proved to be very unreliable.

The Advent of the Cruise Missile

Post-war, the United States Air Force had a number of cruise missile projects under development but many of these were cancelled. Interest reawakened as the Cold War intensified and during the 1950s the United States navy's SSM-N-8 Regulus and the USAF's MGM-1 Matador were both similar to the V1 but nuclear-capable. Between 1957 and 1961, the United States worked on a nuclear-powered cruise missile, Project Pluto, intended to deliver a number of nuclear weapons over targets along its flight path, but this was abandoned when the emphasis moved to inter-continental ballistic missiles (ICBMs).

The early 1980s were a period when the performance of theatre ballistic missiles, as favoured by the Soviet Union, overlapped that of cruise missiles. The Soviet decision to update their theatre missiles led to the United States deploying cruise missiles in Europe for the first time. The Americans did not have a new theatre ballistic missile and saw cruise missiles as being the only effective counter to the Soviet upgrade to retain the balance of power but the decision to deploy led to considerable public controversy.

The Soviet Union had decided that ICBMs were the preferred option for striking at major targets in the West but a range of land-based and air-launched cruise missiles was developed to attack NATO battle groups and at sea submarines were developed to carry cruise missiles and shadow American naval fleets, ready to strike should war break out.

Unlike the V1, cruise missiles were capable of navigating their way to the target and during the war for the liberation of Kuwait from Iraqi control in 1990, high levels of accuracy were achieved. As with the V1, cruise missiles travel at low altitude and the warhead is integrated into the missile so that when it strikes the target and explodes, the missile is lost. Modern cruise missiles can be subsonic, albeit at high subsonic speed, or supersonic. India and Russia have been working jointly on hypersonic cruise missiles, which by definition can travel at least five times the speed of sound, as has the People's Republic of China. These three countries plus Taiwan and France have been developing supersonic cruise missiles, with the French *Air-Sol Moyenne Portée* being an air-launched missile capable of being fitted with a nuclear warhead.

The most numerous cruise missiles in the United States inventory today are the Tomahawk, believed to cost around US$1.5 million each, and the Harpoon, a short-range missile intended for anti-ship strikes. Submarine-launched versions of the Tomahawk with conventional warheads have also been supplied to the Royal Navy but the Tomahawk can also be air-launched or launched from surface vessels.

Storm Shadow is an air-launched Anglo-French-Italian missile intended for use with conventional warheads. Many other nations also have sub-sonic short- and medium-range missiles under development or in production; these include Norway, Turkey, Israel and Iran, as well as the more established producers such as Russia, China and the United States.

The Tomahawk uses a Williams turbofan but can also use a rocket booster as well if submarine- or surface-launched, has a diameter of 20.4 inches (0.52m) and is 18 feet 3 inches (5.56m) long without a booster, with which its length increases to 20 feet 6 inches (6.25m). Wings unfold from the missile after launching and it has a wingspan of 8 feet 9 inches (2.67m). The warhead can be 1,000lb (453kg) and may be conventional or nuclear. Range depends on the variant and whether it is air-, surface- or subsurface-launched but can be up to 1,550 miles (2,495km). It has network-centric warfare capabilities, obtaining target information from aircraft, ships, unmanned aerial vehicles, ground bases or even infantry to locate its target and can also provide information picked up by its sensors to these various sources.

By contrast, the more specialized and shorter-range Harpoon, costing around US$1.2 million, has a diameter of 1.1 feet (0.34m), is 12 feet 3 inches (3.8m) long if air-launched and 15 feet (4.6m) long if launched from a submarine or surface vessel. Its wingspan is 3 feet (0.91m) and the warhead is 488lb (221kg). More than 7,000 of these missiles are in service, mainly with the United States navy and other NATO navies. The range varies, depending on whether it is launched from a ship or an aircraft but can be in excess of 75 miles (121km). A feature of Harpoon is that it can undertake a terminal 'bunt', which is a manoeuvre that sees the surface-skimming missile climb and then fall upon the target.

Storm Shadow can only be air-launched. The name is that used by the Royal Air Force, while to the French it is 'SCALP EG' or *Système de Croisière Autonome a Longue Portée, Emploi Générale*, or long-range general-purpose cruise missile. It is 1.6 feet (0.48m) in diameter and 16.7 feet (5.1m) in length. It carries a 1,000lb (453kg) warhead and is powered by a Turbomeca turbojet. Range is around 160 miles (258km).

Tomahawk has been used by the Royal Navy and United States navy in action off Iraq, while Storm Shadow has been used by the Royal Air Force, French *Armée de l'Air* and the Italian *Aeronautica Militaire* off Libya in 2011.

Chapter 10

The Ballistic Missile

Like the cruise missile, the ballistic missile can trace its origins back to the work of Dr Wernher von Braun at Peenemünde where the V2, another of Hitler's *Vergeltungswaffen* was developed. The V2 was even less accurate than the V1 as it was fired into space with the intention of hitting a target located within a very wide area. It was nevertheless dreaded as there was no warning of its arrival and it was impossible to shoot down.

Officially known as the A-4, work started on the missile in 1933, although from as early as 1919 Robert H. Goddard had been working on liquid-fuelled rockets. Trials began in 1942 but operational use did not start until 8 September 1944 when a V2 hit Chiswick in south-west London, killing three people and injuring another seventeen. It had been launched from a site in The Netherlands, a small flat square of concrete that was easy to conceal and easily repaired if attacked. The V2 was just over 46 feet (14.04m) long but its launching equipment was easily trans-portable. Out of more than 3,000 V2s built, 1,054 were fired at England until the attacks ended on 27 March 1945 with 517, just under an average of three per day, hitting London and killing more than 2,700 people. One of the most serious V2 attacks was shortly before they ended when, in March 1945, a block of flats at Deptford accommodating workers from the Southern Railway and their families was hit, with a quarter of the flats demolished and fifty-one people killed. More than 900 such missiles were fired at the Belgian port of Antwerp. The V2 was able to carry a 2,000lb (907kg) warhead for up to 200 miles (322km).

The V2 was a complicated weapon that was difficult and costly to develop and produce. It was assembled at an underground factory at Nordhausen in the Harz Mountains.

Nuclear Warheads
Work on developing ballistic missiles continued as soon as the war ended. The concept, which means that the longer-range missiles leave the earth's atmosphere and in fact are often described as being sub-orbital before returning to the target, was ideal for the new nuclear weapons as it eliminated the bombers that could be shot down by fighters or anti-

aircraft artillery or missiles. In a massive nuclear attack, there was also the risk of bomber crews being injured by the blast from bombs dropped by others or even of being blinded by the intense flare created by an exploding nuclear weapon.

Not only long-range or intercontinental ballistic missiles (ICBMs) were developed but also shorter-range theatre ballistic missiles, which spent all of their flight within the earth's atmosphere, as did the V2. The range of an ICBM became 5,000 nautical miles (8,900km) or more; intermediate-range ballistic missiles (IRBMs) became 1,500 nautical miles (2,400km) or more; medium-range ballistic missiles (MRBMs) have a range of 500 nautical miles (800km) or more; short-range ballistic missiles (SRBMs) have a range of up to 500 nautical miles (800km). MRBMs and SRBMs have been gradually superseded by cruise missiles. ICBMs, IRBMs and MRBMs are regarded as strategic weapons, while the SRBMs are tactical. At the height of the Cold War, the USSR upgraded its SRBMs in Europe and provoked the USA into deploying cruise missiles for the first time as an upgraded Western deterrent.

The Soviet R-7 *Semyorka* was their first ICBM, while the SM-65 Atlas was the first American version. These early ballistic missiles were fired from hardened silos located in remote areas of the USSR and USA and were set on their course by radio command. The use of radio signals was a significant weakness as electronic countermeasures could jam the signals. More modern ICBMs use inertial guidance which is immune to interference, as well as lightweight and reliable.

Most ICBMs have three stages. The first stage propels the missile into the air and is known as the booster stage; the second sustainer stage takes over for most of the rest of the rocket's trajectory; the third stage comprises the warhead and re-entry which in the ICBMs, as opposed to the shorter-range weapons, also includes a heat shield and penetration aids to help confuse enemy radar.

Using fixed launch bases was another weakness as inevitably their location became known to the enemy. The answer was to place the missiles aboard nuclear-powered submarines. One of the first was the A3 Polaris, known as a submarine-launched ballistic missile (SLBM), used by the United States navy and also provided for the Royal Navy. Each submarine could carry up to sixteen Polaris missiles. Nevertheless, at first the United States hedged its bets by developing another land-based ICBM, the Minuteman, which was developed as a low-cost missile and could be readied for action in just over thirty seconds. The British opted for Polaris and abandoned their own ICBM programme, as well as dropping an advanced stand-off weapon that had encountered development difficulties.

Not only did the Soviet Union also equip its navy with ICBM-carrying nuclear-powered submarines but so too did France, developing its own SLBMs rather than using the US-supplied Polaris, partly because France had excluded itself from NATO's command structure at the time. Nevertheless, the French missiles are really IRBMs rather than ICBMs. The French policy of relying on ICBMs and air-launched missiles is based on the concept that they can 'tear off an arm and a leg' of any enemy, which is regarded as sufficient deterrent for the *Force de Frappe* (strike force). France still maintains a strong force of aircraft capable of delivering nuclear weapons, while the British have abandoned this option and rely completely on SLBMs. The British have always provided their own nuclear and thermonuclear warheads.

A number of other countries have also developed ballistic missiles, sometimes under the cover of conducting space research. These include the People's Republic of China, North Korea and India.

Submarines provide mobile rather than fixed bases and most important of all leave the enemy guessing as to their location. The submarine bases are, of course, vulnerable but in a time of tension any boat (submarines are always referred to as 'boats', not ships) that could be got away would be at sea and even the Royal Navy, with just four ICBM submarines, always has one on patrol at any one time. The number of such craft in the Royal Navy is determined by the need to have a boat on patrol; the original plan was to have a fleet of five but financial considerations meant this could not be achieved. The United States navy has fourteen SLBM-carrying boats, known as SSBNs. The use of a depot ship as opposed to a fixed base also improves the flexibility of a submarine-based system but nuclear-powered submarines cannot be completely independent of fixed bases as these are needed for the complex and time-consuming process of refuelling.

A major step forward was the provision of multiple warheads for ICBMs, which became known as multiple independently-targetable re-entry vehicles (MIRVs) with each missile having two or more MIRVs. In fact, when first introduced to Polaris, three MIRVs were fitted. The advantage of using MIRVs is that more targets can be attacked by a single missile and while the warheads are smaller, this is in line with modern military thinking which is that many smaller warheads are more effective than a single large one. When effective, if any anti-missile defences are deployed, it also means that more warheads are likely to get through. However, some of the MIRVs carried in a missile will be decoys to confuse anti-ballistic missile systems. A peaceful spin-off from the development of MIRVs is the ability of space rockets to put two satellites into orbit from just one launch.

Polaris has now been replaced by the more powerful Trident missile in British and US service, although the US navy had the Poseidon SLBM in service after Polaris was withdrawn and before the first version of Trident was available. Like Polaris, the Trident has MIRVs but the number of these with nuclear warheads has been reduced as part of the general agreement among the original nuclear-armed countries to reduce their numbers.

At one stage the United States considered developing a variant of Trident with conventional warheads, giving it a global strike capability against targets such as terrorist groups that did not warrant a nuclear or these days, thermonuclear, response. This was abandoned largely because of a warning by Russian President Vladimir Putin that firing such a missile could provoke a nuclear response as other countries would not be able to distinguish between an SLBM with conventional warheads and its thermonuclear equivalent.

Chapter 11

Stand-Off Bombs

Another device bequeathed to us by the Second World War is the stand-off bomb, which can be either a glider or 'glide' bomb or a powered missile, depending on the distance from the target at which it is to be released. In dealing with the term 'glide bomb', which means the use of a bomb that can be released from a bomber and glide towards its target, it is important not to be confused with 'glide bombing', which is a term sometimes used to describe shallow-angle dive-bombing.

The Germans did in fact attempt to build a stand-off weapon during the First World War. As early as October 1914, Dr Wilhelm von Siemens proposed a torpedo-glider. This was to be wire-guided and would have utilized a standard naval torpedo fitted with wings. Unlike the stand-off weapons being covered here, it would not have flown into the target but at a suitable distance from the target a signal would be transmitted through the wire that would detach the torpedo from the wings and allow it to drop into the sea and continue towards its target. During flight, the copper wire would carry signals that would enable the airframe component of the weapon to manoeuvre and change course.

This would have been the first wire-guided missile, had it entered operational service. Between January 1915 and August 1918, trials were conducted using an airship as the mother aircraft, sending signals to the torpedo-glider. There were plans to use a heavy bomber but before this could happen the Armistice ended the project.

It seems that little was done between the wars to advance stand-off weapons but remote-controlled glider bombs were developed by the Germans during the Second World War, notably the Ruhrstahl SD 1400, commonly known as the Fritz X, and the Henschel Hs 293. A mother or controlling aircraft would drop the bomb and then use radio control to direct its course towards the target.

As in the First World War, ships were the preferred target. There were several reasons for this. Firstly, accurate targeting was essential as major warships were heavily armoured and bombs could simply bounce off or even break up on hitting the armour. Secondly, by this time warships had acquired increasingly heavy anti-aircraft defences.

The Germans started by fitting a 220lb (100kg) armour-piercing bomb, developed specifically to penetrate the deck armour of battleships, to control surfaces and a radio receiver. The bomber approached the target at high altitude and when within range of it, the bomb was dropped and guided towards the target with spoilers on the rear of the bomb being used to control its rate of descent. It was soon discovered that as the bomb began to slow, the controlling aircraft overtook it and it became difficult to see the bomb. To overcome this, the launch aircraft slowed down after releasing the glider bomb and also started to climb. Even so, the controller had little influence on the angle of descent but after intensive training the most capable controllers were capable, in test drops from 26,000 feet (7,925m), of putting half the bombs within 49 feet (15m) of the target and 90 per cent within 98 feet (30m).

After Italian surrender in 1943, the Luftwaffe sank the battleship *Roma* and damaged the *Italia* using Fritz X bombs. Considerable damage and loss of life was inflicted on the heavy cruiser USS *Savannah*, while the British battleship HMS *Warspite* was hit by three Fritz X bombs and while there were few casualties, she had to be towed to Malta for repairs. She was out of action for six months and one of her turrets was never used again. The light cruiser HMS *Uganda* was hit and put out of action for the rest of the war. Several near misses also damaged the cruiser USS *Philadelphia*.

Although still regarded as a glider bomb, the Henschel Hs 293 had wings and a rocket motor that extended the range at which it could be dropped. Unlike the Fritz X, the Hs 293 did not have an armour-piercing warhead but was intended to be used against slow-moving merchantmen and convoy escorts such as corvettes. A different procedure was followed, with a small liquid-fuelled rocket motor igniting as soon as the glider bomb was dropped and this enabled it to race in front of the bomber, which moved to a course just off to one side of the target, allowing the bomb-aimer to make adjustments as the Hs 293 approached. The trick was to get the range right so that the glider bomb did not fall short of the target.

The Hs 293 was first used on 25 August 1943 over the Bay of Biscay. The sloop HMS *Bideford* was slightly damaged and a member of her crew was killed when hit but the warhead did not detonate properly. Slight damage was also inflicted by a near miss on the sloop HMS *Landguard*. On 27 August an Hs 293 sank HMS *Egret* and seriously damaged HMCS *Athabaskan*.

Orders were given that any ships capable of higher speed were to place themselves between the Hs 293 and its target, to make the controller/bomb-aimer's role more difficult. Fighter patrols were used when available and smokescreens were raised.

The Hs 293 was also used against land targets after the Allied landings in Normandy. In August 1944, it was used against bridges over rivers at the southern end of the Cherbourg Peninsula but with little success. Failure also marked an attempt to use the Hs 293 to stop the Russian advance across the River Oder into Germany.

A special effort was made by the Allies to attack the bases of the German units responsible for using the Hs 293. Radio jammers were also developed to disrupt the radio signal and eventually no fewer than nine different jamming systems were in use in the North Atlantic and the Mediterranean. Even so, the greatest obstacle to the use of the Hs 293 was growing Allied aerial superiority. An attempt to use television guidance met with little success as control inputs produced a jumpy image of the target. A wire-guided version was also developed but never deployed.

The Germans were not the sole designers of glider bombs during the conflict. In the United Kingdom, an air-launched gliding torpedo, the 'Toraplane', and a gliding bomb, the 'Doravane', were both developed. However, the Toraplane could not be launched accurately and was abandoned in 1942.

Greater success was achieved by the United States, where the Aeronca GB-1 was the country's first glider bomb and was used for the first time on 28 May 1944 against the Eifeltor railway marshalling yards in Cologne. The bombs were released at 195 mph, 18 miles (29km) from the target but of 113 glider bombs released, just 42 struck the marshalling yards, killing 82 workers and injuring 1,500. It seems that most spun into the ground and exploded some 15 miles (24km) from the target, possibly because the batteries for the guidance systems failed to hold their charge.

Nevertheless, the Americans persevered with the GB series of glider bombs, with later versions including some guided by television with contrast-seekers for anti-shipping use, while the GB-8 was guided by a controller and the Felix glider bomb was guided towards the target by infrared.

The glider bomb was not the monopoly of the United States Army Air Forces as the United States navy also used these weapons, including the 'Bat' and the 'Pelican'. The Bat used an active radar-seeker but when used in the Pacific for the first time on 13 August 1944 failed to distinguish targets in a cluttered environment and soon proved susceptible to simple radar countermeasures.

The Japanese took a different approach, using piloted glider bombs with rocket assistance. These were a variant of the *kamikaze* suicide bombers. Known as the *Oka* ('cherry blossom'), these were small rocket-powered aircraft which could fly for up to 11 miles, using five small rockets, before gliding or diving onto the target with a 2,600lb (1,180kg) warhead. Of flimsy wooden construction, the *Oka* was carried within range of the target by a land-based bomber. Sometimes the pilot flew in the mother plane until close to the target when he climbed down into the *Oka* before it was released but on other occasions he spent the entire time in the *Oka*. The problem with this heavyweight design was that a large and not very manoeuvrable bomber had to get past increasingly strong Allied fighter defences.

A fundamental problem for the Japanese, not just with the *Oka* but with the *kamikaze* missions generally, was that many of the pilots were inexperienced and often had little more than sufficient training for them to reach the target. It was also the case that many had poor ship recognition skills, often mistaking tankers for aircraft carriers and cruisers for battleships.

Smart Bombs

Post-war development concentrated mainly on improving guidance systems and for many years the manned bomber was still expected to reach the target. Many of these stand-off weapons became known as 'smart bombs' and during the Vietnam War they succeeded in reducing US combat aircraft losses as well as improving accuracy, particularly against targets such as bridges. Among the more successful were the USAF's AGM-62 Walleye and the AGM-65 Maverick missile. These used contrast seekers but during the 1980s, laser guidance and systems using global positioning (GPS) became more commonplace. Television-based systems have all but been replaced by the new technology but remain important when absolute accuracy is needed. Improved anti-aircraft defences, usually missile-based, made the use of such weapons necessary. The variety of targets considered suitable for such weapons also increased, with many air forces in Europe using stand-off weapons incorporating cluster bombs to attack air bases and inflict heavy damage on runways and taxi-ways. Anti-shipping weapons also remained important.

A typical missile such as the AGM-12 Bullpup, used by many NATO air forces including the Royal Air Force and Royal Navy, was guided to the target by the launch aircraft using flares fitted to the missile which were kept in line with the target. Powered by a liquid-propellant rocket, the Bullpup could deliver a variety of warheads including high-explosive, high-fragmentation or even nuclear.

Larger and more powerful was the British Hawker Siddeley Dynamics Blue Steel, a liquid-fuelled rocket with a range of up to 200 miles (322km) when launched by a Hawker Siddeley Vulcan bomber at high altitude to carry a thermonuclear warhead to the target. When the RAF switched to a strategy of low-level attack to avoid enemy radar detection, the range of the missile was considerably reduced.

An increasingly common application for stand-off missiles is the destruction of enemy air defence radars, using anti-radiation missiles that home in onto the radar transmitters.

The dividing line between stand-off weapons and cruise missiles became increasingly blurred as the capabilities of the weapons increased. The jet-powered AGM-28 Hound Dog entered service with the USAF in 1960 and was capable of Mach 2.1, around 1,500 mph (2,400 kmph), carrying a thermonuclear warhead weighing 1,742lb (790kg) over a distance of up to 785 miles (1,263km). A novel feature was that the missile was capable of a 'dog-leg' attack, flying to a pre-set location in the hope of drawing enemy fighters away from the target, then turning and flying on to the target. Later versions had a reduced radar cross-section to make detection more difficult. The AGM-28 Hound Dog was retired from service in the late 1970s.

One weapon that remains true to the original glider-bomb concept is the AGM-154 Joint Standoff Weapon (JSOW) in use by the USAF and US navy, as well as a number of NATO air forces. Currently in service, this is unpowered and at 160 inches (4.1m) long with a wingspan of 106 inches (269cm) can be dropped from a fighter aircraft such as the Lockheed F-16. The range is 14 miles (23km) if dropped at low altitude, rising to 81 miles (130km) if dropped at high altitude. It is a 'fire-and-forget' weapon, using a combination of GPS and INS (inertial navigation system) and can be used at night or in bad weather. A variety of warheads can be fitted: the AGM-154A has bomblets in its warhead both for armour penetration and incendiary effects; the AGM-154B has anti-armour-piercing bomblets that use infrared to detect their targets; and the AGM-154C has the Broach two-stage weapon to penetrate hardened targets.

Chapter 12

Surface-to-Air Missiles

Even before the First World War, concerns were expressed that an aircraft dropping bombs over enemy territory could be fired upon. Some even thought that this would be a reason not to drop bombs! The First World War soon saw bombing become an accepted tactic, even a strategy, although the first bombs had been dropped earlier during the Balkan Wars by Italian pilots. The earliest bombs were crude artillery shells fitted with stabilizing fins, as was bomb-aiming with the bomb dropped over the side of an aircraft or airship, but bombs soon became more powerful and their aiming more effective. In the United Kingdom, the Royal Navy was initially responsible for anti-aircraft gunnery in and around London but eventually this duty passed to the British army, where it stayed during the two world wars.

As aircraft began to fly higher and faster, anti-aircraft artillery became less effective, although this did not become a major problem until late in the Second World War by which time Allied air superiority was such that the concept was not accorded any priority. The problem was, of course, that anti-aircraft gunnery was not always able to hit the target and as aircraft became higher-flying and larger shells were needed, the rate of fire became slower.

A good example of the problem in practice was that the German 88mm guns, which were regarded as being among the finest, if not the best, during the Second World War, needed an average of 2,805 rounds to hit a high-flying Boeing B-17 Fortress. When the B-29 Superfortress entered the war against Japan, the problem became even more acute. Fighters could not reach the aircraft unless stripped of all their guns and so another version of the *kamikaze* suicide pilot was born, one who had to fly his aircraft into a B-29. Unless there was a lucky shot that struck a vital part of the aircraft – ideally the pilots (or pilot, as the British heavy bombers had a single pilot due to personnel shortages and the time taken for training) – it took more than a single hit by flak to disable, let alone destroy, a heavy bomber.

The Germans used a different approach. They invented what was really the world's first true interceptor, the Messerschmitt Me 163 *Komet*, a rocket-powered aircraft that first flew in 1944. A single Walter liquid-fuelled rocket powered the aircraft, which could reach a speed of 500 mph (800 kmph) and had an endurance of eight minutes, although this could be extended by being towed into position or by intermittent gliding. Take-off was normally by catapult and landing used a skid instead of a wheeled undercarriage.

The concept of a rocket was well-known by the time the first aeroplane had flown, having been introduced to Europe by Congreve more than a hundred years earlier and used at the Second Battle of Copenhagen. It was not until 1925 that the idea of an anti-aircraft missile was first mooted. This was, confusingly in the light of later developments, known as a 'beam-riding missile' but unlike later surface-to-air missiles (SAMs), the beam was not a radar beam but the beam of a searchlight. A selenium cell would be mounted on each of the rocket's four tail fins with the cell facing backwards and when any one of the cells lost the searchlight beam, it would move the rocket in the opposite direction back into the beam. This was never built and in fact seems not to have been favoured with even a diagram. In 1931, Dr Gustav Rasmus produced a design for a rocket that would home in on the sound of an aircraft's engines. This was never built and its homing sensors could have been confused by the engines of the many bombers present in a major air-raid.

Nevertheless, the limitations of traditional anti-aircraft fire were recognized as early as 1942 when Walther von Axthelm predicted that soon 'aircraft speeds and flight altitudes will gradually reach 625 mph and between 33,000 and 49,000 feet'.

During the Second World War, the Germans were soon considering surface-to-air missiles. In February 1941, Friederich Halder proposed a concept known as a 'flak rocket' and Wernher von Braun was asked to consider a guided missile capable of reaching an altitude of between 50,000 to 60,000 feet (15,240 to 18,288m). Von Braun believed that a better solution would be a manned rocket-powered interceptor, as the Me 163 turned out to be, but the Luftwaffe's anti-aircraft artillery leaders were uninterested in a manned aircraft and in the resultant arguments between the proponents of the different solutions, almost two years were wasted.

Nevertheless, work was being done behind the scenes and as early as 1940 a rocket called the *Feuerlilie* was proposed and followed in 1941 by the *Wasserfall* and Henschel's Hs 117 *Schmetterling*. Ideas were one thing but development was something else and this did not begin in earnest until the Allied air-raids became much heavier and more concentrated in

1943. New rockets were designed at this time, including the *Enzian* and the *Rheintochter* as well as the unguided *Taifun*, which was designed to be launched as a rocket barrage against the bomber formations. This was a tactic used by North Vietnam against USAF bomber formations during the Vietnam War.

Some of these missiles were designed to be launched in advance of a bomber formation and then fly towards them on a head-on approach, which it was hoped would at least break up the formations. The others, such as the *Wasserfall* and *Rheintochter*, were supersonic and radio-controlled, flying directly at their chosen targets from below while the controllers either directed them by eye or by comparing the radar returns of the missile and the target on a single radar screen. However, rather than concentrating resources on a single system, all were developed at the same time and by the time Germany surrendered, none was ready for operational use. This was despite Germany's industrial genius, Albert Speer, supporting the projects and his belief that had development started as soon as the designs were produced and followed through, the deva-stating bomber raids of 1944 could have been fought off. In fact, Speer's confidence may have been over-optimism because the growing size of British and American bomber raids was a tactic intended to overwhelm the defences and while missiles might have been more effective than flak, they were very much more expensive to produce than artillery shells.

Both the leading Allied powers also worked on surface-to-air missiles during the war. The British developed unguided anti-aircraft rockets early in the war, using the code name 'Z-Battery', but as Allied aerial superiority grew, interest waned and the project was shelved. Interest was rekindled with the arrival of the Henschel Hs 293 glide bombs and Fritz X anti-shipping missiles, both of which were launched at some distance from the target and out of range of its AA weapons.

In the United States, Operation BUMBLEBEE was launched to build a ramjet-powered missile that would destroy a missile-carrying aircraft at long range, which initially was regarded as a distance of up to 10 miles (16km) and an altitude of 30,000 feet (9,144m). It was estimated that a war-head of between 300 and 600lb would have a 30 to 60 per cent chance of success. Interest in such defensive weapons grew with the start of the intense *kamikaze* suicide attacks at Leyte Gulf and the Battle of Okinawa. The British responded by developing two missiles – the Fairey Stooge and Brakemine – while the US worked on the SAM-N-2 Lark but the latter proved impossible to develop satisfactorily and was never used, while the

British missiles were not available until the war was over and were then used for research.

The one real success of the wartime SAM development came out of Operation BUMBLEBEE and the missile, which entered service as the RIM-8 Talos, took sixteen years to enter service.

The limitations of anti-aircraft guns were already accepted by the armed forces of the leading nations. Work on surface-to-air missiles continued after the war and intensified as jet bombers were introduced in large numbers.

The First SAM
Work began in 1944 on a project that was first tested in 1952 as the Nike Ajax and became operational in 1954 in the United States army. This was the first fully-operational surface-to-air guided missile but as the first generation, concerns were soon raised about its ability to deal with a large bomber formation. The result was an upgraded development known as the Nike Hercules when it entered service in 1958 and for the first time this SAM could carry a nuclear warhead, enabling it to destroy many bombers at once if flying in formation.

The USAAF also had its own project for a weapon that would hit an attacking bomber head-on. In 1946 this was launched as Project Thumper but was later merged with another project, Wizard, and eventually emerged for service with what had become the United States Air Force in 1959 as the CIM-10 Bomarc. This had an astonishing range of more than 300 miles (483km) but was very expensive and, even worse, its reliability was poor.

While the UK had enjoyed some success with its wartime developments, the momentum dropped at the end of the war, only to pick up again as the growing threat posed by the Soviet Union and the newly-created Warsaw Pact came to be recognized. A new air defence system was planned, just as the Chain Home radar system had revolutionized the nation's defences before the outbreak of the Second World War. New radars, jet fighters and missiles began to be introduced. The Royal Air Force received the Bristol Bloodhound in 1958 and the British army the English Electric Thunderbird the following year. It took slightly longer to introduce surface-to-air guided missiles to ships at sea; partly because of limitations on space and, of course, while this first generation of guided missiles tended to be quite large, there was also the need to be able to install radar and control systems. The Royal Navy received its Hawker Siddeley Sea Slug in 1961, fired from a position at the stern of the ship, ready for service aboard its County-class* guided missile destroyers which also broke ground by being the first British destroyers with a helicopter hangar and landing platform enabling them to operate the Westland Wessex, a licence-built turboshaft-powered development of the Sikorsky S-58.

Work in the Soviet Union does not seem to have started until after the end of the Second World War. As the Cold War intensified and wartime allies became peacetime enemies, the Russians were concerned that they might face heavy bomber formations of up to 1,000 aircraft such as the RAF had sent to Berlin during the war. The initial answer was the S-25 *Berkut* system, known to NATO as the SA-1 and which entered service in 1955, with Moscow being ringed by these missiles the following year. This was followed by the S-75 *Divina*, known to NATO as the SA-2, which entered service in 1957. Unlike the SA-1, this was highly portable and sufficiently ahead of its time to remain in service for more than forty years.

Not all the early activity was in the United States, the United Kingdom or the Soviet Union. In Switzerland, Oerlikon started work on the RSD58 in 1947; it was available in 1952 but never entered service, although a number were sold for research and training purposes.

The Vietnam War was the first in which SAMs were used, with some 17,000 Soviet technicians seconded to the North Vietnamese armed forces which received almost 8,000 SAMs and conducted nearly 6,000 launches. While this was supposedly one of the Cold War proxy conflicts with US forces initially sent as 'advisers' to the South Vietnamese, between 1963 and 1966 American losses were due to the efforts of Soviet personnel rather than North Vietnamese forces. After suffering heavy losses, the Americans soon learned the value of using stand-off weapons which in any case soon proved to be more accurate. The large Boeing B-52 bombers proved particularly vulnerable, especially as the Vietnamese often launched missiles in salvoes, making escape difficult. One lesson of the war was that high-altitude flight was no longer practical but instead was almost suicidal as the aircraft presented a clear target long enough for missile radar systems to lock onto it.

Research into missiles continued unabated and air force tactics began to change. Not only was there greater use of stand-off missiles of one kind or

---

*Often regarded as cruisers because of their size and tonnage, the County-class vessels were nevertheless destroyers, having a 4.5-inch main armament and, of course, destroyer 'D' pennant numbers.

another but aircraft were developed that could fly low, 'under the radar net', so as to avoid detection until the last minute. As low flying used more fuel and decreased the operational radius, what became known as 'hi-lo-lo-hi' tactics became the norm, meaning that an aircraft would fly high on leaving its base, drop to a low altitude for the attack, start its homeward journey still flying low and then climb again once clear of enemy defences. Aircraft were developed that could handle this demanding profile, such as the American F-111 and A-6 and the British Buccaneer, followed by the Anglo-German-Italian Panavia Tornado GR series (the latter aircraft also had an interceptor variant).

This change in tactics necessitated a change in missile defences. Large heavyweight missiles were no longer appropriate, no matter how long their range or how powerful their warheads. The need was for smaller missiles with high speed that could intercept an aircraft as it closed upon its target. These missiles, being lighter, were also portable. The first self-contained mobile SAM with everything mounted on one vehicle was the Soviet *Osa*, known as the SA-8 to NATO, but others followed including the MIM-23 Hawk in the USA, the Rapier in the UK and the Roland and Crotale in France.

At Sea
At sea, the problem was slightly different as the navies equipped with sea-skimming missiles. An early answer to these was the Royal Navy's Short Sea Cat, a wire-guided variant that replaced the 40mm cannon aboard British warships including the highly-successful *Leander*-class general-purpose frigates and was the first operational point-defence SAM. A military version was the Tiger Cat, also by Short Brothers. This was followed by the American Sperry RIM-7 Sea Sparrow. The Sea Cat was followed by the BAe Sea Wolf, with a radar capable of detecting a 4.5-inch shell.

The next logical step in SAM development was the MANPAD (man-portable air-defence) system which could be used by a trained infantry-man. This was a concept identified during the Second World War by the Germans, who designed the *Fliegerfaust* which never entered service. It would have been of limited value had it done so as the weapon would have been of little use against the new jet aircraft.

Technology for the man-portable SAM was not ready until the 1960s. The United States introduced the FIM-43 Redeye, the British the Blowpipe and the Russians the SA-7 Grail. These were followed by improved missiles such as the FIM-92 Stinger, 9K34 *Strela*-3 known to NATO as the

SA-14, and the British Starstreak, while the Chinese developed their first MANPAD, the FN-6.

These missiles have become a cause for concern as MANPADs have found their way into the armoury of terrorist groups, sometimes due to revolution and sometimes because these were supplied during the Cold War to unstable regimes. Throughout much of the world the fear is that such missiles could be used to down commercial aircraft in an act of terrorism. In areas of high risk, aircraft can be fitted with defensive measures but wholesale fitting would be costly and also difficult to justify as aircraft are most at risk on the approach and as one defensive measure is the use of flares, would be dangerous and impractical when approaching an airport surrounded by an urban area.

Chapter 13

Jet Engines

One Second World War innovation that has affected the lives of many people has been the jet engine. The all-embracing term 'jet engine' is in fact misleading as there are no fewer than five different types: the turbojet, the ram jet, the turboprop, the turboshaft and the turbofan. A more recent development has been the scramjet, capable of hypersonic speeds; i.e. speeds in excess of Mach 5 or more than 3,000 mph (4,800 kmph).

Some maintain that rocket motors should also be considered as a form of jet engine since the rocket's thrust acts in the same way as a jet engine but instead of air-breathing, the rocket has oxygen added to its fuel. There is a sound case for this but the rocket pre-dates the jet engine and even pre-dates the aeroplane.

Around 100 BC, Hero of Alexandria demonstrated the effect of thrust using a rotating boiler which, filled with water and suspended above a fire, rotated as steam escaped from four nozzles but it was not until 1842 that W.H. Phillips built a model steam-powered helicopter with rotor-tip steam jets, which flew across two fields. Fuel for this machine was a mixture of charcoal, nitre and gypsum. However, there was no attempt to build a full-sized, practicable machine.

In 1791, Englishman John Barber was awarded a patent for a stationary gas turbine. However, the first attempt at running a practical machine was in 1903 when Norwegian Aegidius Elling succeeded but the engineering of the day and the materials available meant that this could not enter production. A patent was awarded to Frenchman Maxime Guillaume in 1921 for an axial-flow turbojet, which encouraged Britain's Royal Aircraft Establishment to start experimental work.

The start of a more sustained approach leading to a practical jet engine was in 1928 when a cadet at the Royal Air Force College at Cranwell, Frank Whittle, put forward his ideas for a turbojet. The following year he developed his ideas further and in January 1930, he made his first patent application, which was awarded in 1932. By 1937, Whittle had his first engine running, liquid-fuelled, but was unable to interest the government in the concept so work continued slowly. One early problem encountered on a test run with the first engine was that it started to accelerate and would not stop, even when it seemed that all of the fuel had been used. Subsequent inspection showed that the fuel had leaked into the engine, settling in pools, and the engine would not stop until all the fuel had been burned off.

The First Jets

Meanwhile, Hans von Ohain had started work in Germany in 1935, unaware of Whittle's progress. His first engine was less advanced than Whittle's and would only run under external power using liquid hydrogen as a fuel but he was able to demonstrate the concept to Ernst Heinkel, one of Germany's leading aircraft manufacturers. Subsequent work developed a version of the engine using gasoline. A simple aircraft, the small He 178, was designed and built to test what became known as the Hirth HeS 3 variant of Ohain's work and this was flown by Erich Warsitz on 27 August 1939: the world's first jet aeroplane flight.

Work then continued at the engine division of another German aircraft manufacturer, Junkers, leading to the production Jumo 004 jet engine that would power the world's first jet fighter, the Messerschmitt Me 262, and the world's first jet bomber, the Arado Ar 234. Yet Hitler's insistence on using the Me 262 as a bomber meant that it was never given the chance to prove itself in the front line until it was too late for the aircraft to make a difference.

Back in the United Kingdom, the authorities finally began to realize that Whittle had an important invention. The first British jet aircraft, the Gloster E28/39, sometimes known as the Gloster 'Whittle', flew for the first time on 15 May 1941. Experience with this aircraft led to the development of the twin-engine Gloster Meteor jet fighter, which entered service with the RAF in July 1944.

Post-war, the Allies examined Ohain's engines and while many lessons were learned, the United Kingdom also provided engines for the United States and the USSR.

Although piston-engined fighters were still being developed, interest switched rapidly from these and by the early 1950s most fighters were jet-powered. Initially there was some scepticism among naval aviators because of the low rate of acceleration but the advent of the steam catapult overcame this and as the aircraft developed, the initial problem of short range was overcome.

The Main Jet Engine Types

Both Whittle and Ohain had produced the turbojet, the original type of jet engine in which three sets of rotating blades are used: the first set draws air into the engine, the second compresses the air, and after fuel is injected and ignited, the third set are driven by the hot and high-pressure efflux to power the first two sets of blades. The fact that all moving parts worked in the same direction, unlike the up-and-down movement of pistons in the original internal combustion engines, meant that the jet engine was simpler and also brought increased reliability as well as power. Piston engines with propellers were also becoming much less efficient as speeds increased.

Ramjets are the simplest forms of jet engine, as they have no moving parts at all and consist simply of a jet pipe into which fuel is injected and ignited. This means that a ramjet cannot function unless air is flowing through the engine at sufficient speed. Ramjets make suitable engines for missiles dropped from aircraft or ones that have been boosted to operational speed by rockets. A number of military aircraft have used ramjets to boost their speed, including the Lockheed Neptune, a piston-engined maritime-reconnaissance aircraft. Much more common today is the use of ramjets to boost the speed of military aircraft, with the ramjet placed at the end of the jet pipe and further heating the efflux or exhaust gases in a process known as 'reheat' or 'afterburning'. The bright orange glow sometimes seen from the rear of a military aircraft shows that reheat is in use and performance figures for such engines are quoted as either 'dry', i.e. without reheat, or with reheat.

Two commercial aircraft have used reheat: the Anglo-French Concorde supersonic airliner and its competitor, the Soviet Tupolev Tu-144. Concorde used turbojets and as a result was capable of 'super-cruising'; i.e. maintaining supersonic speed without the use of reheat and the extra fuel consumption that entails. The Tu-144 had to use reheat to maintain supersonic speed as it used turbofan engines that lacked sufficient power at high altitudes for high-speed flight. Concorde only used reheat to accelerate through the sound barrier.

Early jet engines were uneconomic at low and medium altitudes and also needed lengthy runways. This gave the piston engine a stay of execution when runways or distances were short or low flying was involved, as with smaller or short-haul airliners and maritime-reconnaissance aircraft. The need to bring jet reliability to such operations resulted in the development of the turboprop, in which a propeller was combined with a jet engine with a gearbox between the two so that the fast rotation of the jet was reduced before being transmitted to the propeller. The first successful turboprop airliner to enter service was the British Vickers Viscount.

The turboprop was quick to prove itself for applications when a speed of up to 400 mph (640 kmph) was sufficient and most turboprop aircraft were much slower than this. Passengers welcomed the lack of vibration, an inherent feature of powerful piston engines. However, turboprops usually require more maintenance than a pure jet engine because of the need to have a gearbox between the power plant and the propeller or airscrew.

While early helicopters were notoriously difficult to maintain and offered limited performance, the usefulness of vertical take-off and the ability to hover soon showed that these were more than just novelty machines. A significant step forward in reliability and performance came with the introduction of the turboshaft, basically a turboprop adapted for use in helicopters. Some piston-engined helicopters were modified for use with turboshafts but soon helicopters emerged that were designed for the new power plant and designers had the opportunity to create twin-engined and even three-engined helicopters, improving performance and reliability still further.

Growing public concern over aircraft noise, especially as aircraft became bigger and far more commonplace, as well as fuel consumption as the price of crude oil began to rise, led to the development of the turbofan. Early attempts to reduce aircraft noise led to various modifications of the tail pipe, largely to mix air with the efflux. The turbofan took exactly the opposite course, instead increasing the size of the first-stage fan so that a proportion of the air went around rather than through the engine. This reduced noise and improved fuel consumption, as well as performance at lower altitudes. The technology, as with turboprops and turboshafts, gradually became available on smaller engines but also saw larger engines developed with some having first-stage fans with a wider circumference than the fuselages of small airliners.

The drawback of the turbofan, as with the piston engine and the turboprop, is that performance reduces at higher altitudes. Nevertheless, the reductions in noise and fuel consumption and the greater reliability of ever-larger engines are benefits that have meant that today all new airliners are either turbofans or turboprops, with high-speed turboprops being able to match jet schedules on short-distance routes.

Non-Aviation Applications

The use of the jet engine has spread from aviation into other areas. Initially attempts were made to apply it to motor vehicles by Rover in the

United Kingdom and by Brown Boveri in Switzerland to railway loco-motives. In both cases, thirst and poor acceleration ruined the jet's chances of becoming the power plant of choice on the roads and on the railways.

Greater success was found for the jet, as the gas turbine, in electricity production, usually in power stations serving a small market or when emergency additional power was needed immediately.

At sea, the jet or gas turbine engine became popular with the world's leading navies. At first, it was often used as a back-up to steam turbines in a system known as COSAG (combined steam and gas) and had the same benefit in naval applications of providing power instantly, instead of the delay in firing-up boilers and waiting for them to reach steam-generating temperature. Other navies found CODAG (combined diesel and gas) a more economical solution and some, including the Royal Navy, had a number of classes of warship that were completely gas turbine-powered. A small number of gas turbine-powered ferries were built for use across the Baltic but during a fuel crisis in the early 1970s, these proved too expensive to operate.

While cost seems to have inhibited some applications for the gas turbine, the paradox is that it has made a significant contribution to reducing the cost of air travel, to the extent that in the developed world air travel is an everyday means of transport and people have come to speak of the 'jet age' as their grandfathers would have spoken of the 'steam age'. In fact, in some countries an air journey of 400 miles (644km) or so is often cheaper than making the same journey by train. Reasons for this include the greater productivity of jet aircraft, both because of their speed and because they are far bigger than the piston-engined aircraft of the past. Overall, fuel prices have also fallen.

While jet engines can run on gasoline, the preferred fuel is kerosene, similar to paraffin in nature and known in commercial applications as JP4 or Jet-P. This is heavier than gasoline but today it is also cheaper. However, a major factor for its almost universal adoption is safety. Anxious to demonstrate this at a time when both types of fuel were being used, Lord Brabazon of Tiara, a British pioneer of flight and air minister at the time, poured out an amount of kerosene, stood in the puddle, lit a match and dropped it into the puddle and after it had fizzled out, challenged anyone to do the same with gasoline. Not only is the flashpoint of kerosene much higher than that of gasoline, it does not explode upon ignition.

Chapter 14

Helicopters

It took some forty years from the first aeroplane flight by the Wright brothers for the practical helicopter to emerge. While the first helicopters were frail machines with limited speed and carrying potential, there was nonetheless no doubt that the helicopter was meeting a long-felt need, that of vertical take-off and landing. Even better, the helicopter could hover in mid-air and even move backwards or sideways if necessary, although at far less speed than in forward flight.

There was nothing new about the concept but making it a reality was a major problem. The technical difficulties were such that even today, the helicopter is generally more expensive to buy and fly than a conventional fixed-wing aircraft and more difficult as well.

At first, many pioneers thought that the helicopter would be a short cut to powered flight and even confused with the alleged benefits of the ornithopter, which was supposed to achieve flight by emulating birds and flapping its wings. Such pioneers had no conception of the advantages the helicopter would bring and none of the problems of control inherent in the helicopter. Rotation of the wings, as in a helicopter which is, as a result, technically known as a rotary-wing aircraft, was seen as a substitute following their inability to design and build a satisfactory flapping wing.

Balloons and gliders pre-dated the helicopter but even these milestones along the way to powered heavier-than-air flight were still far from reality when the Italian artist, Leonardo da Vinci, produced what has since become known as the first design for a helicopter at some time around 1500. Leonardo's helicopter was to consist of a simple helical screw powered by a clockwork motor. Like other aspiring aircraft designers, Leonardo also produced designs for man-powered ornithopters.

Rather more practical was a design by two Frenchmen, Launoy and Bienvenue, in 1784 (the year after the first balloon ascents) for a small helicopter with two rotors at either end of a shaft powered by a bowstring. The limitations were obvious; however, it was constructed and became the basis for a successful toy.

Given the delay in achieving helicopter flight, it was not surprising that the applications for a helicopter appeared before the machine itself. The arrival of first the hot-air balloon and then the hydrogen balloon within weeks of one another in 1783 soon led to the captive or tethered observation balloon being used by the military. The first recorded use of the balloon for artillery-spotting from the air came in 1794 at the Siege of Maubeuge, shortly followed by the use of balloons for the Siege of Charleroi and the Battle of Fleurus.

Another application for the helicopter, that of airborne assault, appeared in a cartoon produced during the Napoleonic Wars, depicting extremely large balloons carrying an invasion force of men and horses across the English Channel from France to England.

The helicopter even defeated that most imaginative and successful early pioneer, Yorkshireman Sir George Cayley, who designed a model helicopter in 1796 when he was just 23 years old. This was his first design and was similar to that of Launoy and Bienvenue. He then abandoned work on helicopter design for several years until in 1843 he produced a design for an 'aerial carriage'. This was a compound helicopter with lift from four revolving wings, mounted biplane-fashion on either side of the fuselage, and propulsion from a tail-mounted rotor.

Cayley was a prolific inventor and social reformer who produced inventions aimed at improving railway safety as well as designing the ideal form of a fixed-wing aeroplane and identifying many of the problems that had to be overcome before powered flight would be possible. He was responsible for the first manned flights, sending a small boy and later an adult, his coachman, on glides across a valley.

Another design that showed some promise was that of the Englishman W.H. Phillips, who built a steam-powered model helicopter with rotor-tip steam jets using a fuel of mixed charcoal, nitre and gypsum which actually managed to fly across two fields, although their size remains unknown. His fellow countryman, Bourne, built and tested a number of clockwork-powered model helicopters based on Launoy and Bienvenue's concept.

In France, Vicomte Ponton d'Amécourt experimented with clockwork models and while his first in 1861 was a failure, many of those that followed, all with contra-rotating rotors, flew very well. One of his models even had a parachute fitted so it could land safely after the clockwork mechanism wound down. The use of contra-rotating rotors solved the problem of the fuselage spinning hopelessly and fatally on its own rotor. Also in France, Gabriel de la Landelle produced a design for an aerial ship with large steam-powered rotors that may have influenced Jules Verne's *Clipper of the Clouds*, published in 1886. De la Landelle's lasting contribution to aviation was coining the words 'aviation' and 'aviator', although of course to him they were *l'aviation* and *l'aviateur*.

Another French design was the Paucton Pterophore that appeared in 1868, with two large rotors or 'pterophores', one of which provided lift and the other was used for forward movement. It was fortunate that this design never left the drawing board as 'propulsion' was to be provided by a man-powered crank! Six years later, Wilheim von Achenbach produced a design that showed some promise as the large rotor for lift was accompanied by a smaller rotor to counter the main rotor's rotational effects but the complicated design also included other small rotors for steering and propulsion. It too was never built.

There were three more significant attempts at designing a helicopter before the nineteenth century was out. In 1877 Emmanuel Dieuaide produced a design with a contra-rotating rotor, as did Forlanini in 1878, when the Frenchman Castel produced a co-axial rotor design. Dieuaide's design was meant to be steam-powered and he overcame the problem of heavy boilers by having steam piped from large boilers on the ground; a novel idea but one that would have limited the machine to a very small area. Forlanini also believed in steam power but had the boiler pre-heated on the ground before attaching it to the helicopter so that the steam could flow into the pistons. Completely impractical for a large helicopter, the Forlanini did at least rise to 42 feet (13m) in trials with a model. Other designers tinkered with different forms of propulsion, including rubberband power.

A missed opportunity occurred in 1904 when C. Renard advocated flapping rotor blades without realizing that this was the simplest solution to the problem of the rotor blades advancing and retreating on opposite sides, with the advancing proportion rising to dissipate the additional lift and the retreating portion falling. Instead, Renard seems to have viewed his idea as a simplified means of achieving ornithoptering flight.

The idea of using the rotor blades for directional control, now known as cyclic pitch control, was suggested by Crocco in 1906 but it was left to Ellehammer to demonstrate its use. This was probably the only success of the unfortunate Ellehammer's career.

The need to be able to see more of the battlefield was such that one way of avoiding the cumbersome balloons, which had to be inflated before use, was the man-carrying kite. These were experimented with, especially in the UK, by the American Samuel Cody on behalf of the British army.

The first aeroplane flights in 1903 preceded some more hopeful designs but still far short of a practical helicopter. In France, Louis Breguet and

Richet built a full-sized helicopter test rig at Douai that finally succeeded in making a tentative man-carrying tethered flight on 29 September 1907, using a 50hp Antoinette engine which drove four rotors. On 13 November of that year, Paul Cornu actually flew a helicopter with two laterally offset rotor blades powered by a 24hp Antoinette engine. Breguet then concentrated on fixed-wing aircraft.

The talented Russian designer Igor Sikorsky built two helicopters at Kiev in the Ukraine in 1909 and 1910 using co-axial rotors and achieved lift, although still far short of a sustained flight. Oddly, in view of his later work, he then abandoned helicopters and concentrated on building what were large aircraft designs for the day, known as 'airbuses', before fleeing the Bolshevik Revolution to work in the United States on amphibians and flying boats.

A number of other impractical designs followed during the First World War and after. In 1918, the United States Army's Air Service Engineering Division considered a helicopter design by Peter Cooper-Hewitt and drew attention to the potential of vertical take-off for restricted landing areas. The following year, the US army conducted tests with a quarter-scale McWhirter 'Autoplane'. That same year, Russian *émigré* George de Bothezat approached the army offering to build a helicopter and was awarded a contract worth US$20,000 (£5,000 at the then exchange rate), which was paid in instalments. The helicopter was ready by late 1920 and had four rotors, each with six blades, mounted on diagonal cross-members, with the pilot sitting in the middle where the cross-members met. The first flight was on 18 December 1921 at Mount Cook Field, rising to a height of 6 feet (1.8m) and remaining there for two minutes moving with the breeze for about 300 feet (91m) before descending and running into the perimeter fence.

This was an encouraging start and in 1923 the helicopter was able to take off with two men but despite replacing the original 180hp Le Rhone rotary engine with a more powerful 220hp engine, the De Bothezat remained an impractical and experimental machine due to the limitations of its performance and its complexity. Meanwhile, in 1922, Henry Berliner produced a machine that made a tethered flight for the United States army but was still nothing more than a novelty.

The Autogiro
Nevertheless, all of this activity culminated in what might be described as an interim solution in a hybrid between the conventional aeroplane and the helicopter in what became known as the gyroplane, although the leading builder, Spaniard Juan de la Cierva, marketed them as autogiros.

The first successful autogiro flight was at Getafe in Spain in 1922 after earlier experiments using modified Avro biplanes. De la Cierva modified Renard's solution, allowing the rotors to flap on a simple hinge. The autogiro did not have a mainplane other than a short non-lifting stub to carry the ailerons and at last the rotors genuinely acted as wings. A conventional tractor propeller was fitted to the fuselage and the rotor blades rotated freely in the slipstream from the propeller. Take-off was short rather than vertical, with the aircraft running forward before hopping into the air. On 9 January 1923, Lieutenant Alejandro Gomez Spencer made the first flight and the machine was subsequently demonstrated at Cuatro Vientos.

In 1925, De la Cierva moved to England and became a naturalized British citizen. It was in England in 1933 that he produced an advance on his basic design by introducing a semi-vertical 'jump-start'. He did this by inserting a drive from the engine to the blades and as the engine powered up, turned the rotor blades into positive pitch so that the machine jumped up to 30 feet (9m) into the air before the drive to the rotor blades was disconnected and the machine progressed in normal autogiro flight. Despite this, De la Cierva was not so much interested in vertical take-off but in making flight safer by removing the risk of a stall during take-off and the initial climb.

Produced under licence by Avro as the Rota, the autogiro was soon being built under licence in the United States by Pitcairn and also by French and Italian manufacturers. In 1931, a Pitcairn autogiro made the first deck landing on a ship, while in 1935 Wing Commander Brie of the RAF made a series of landings aboard a British cruiser.

Possibly if the economic climate had been better and defence budgets not pared to the bone, more progress might have been made and the autogiro developed into the compound helicopter. Louis Breguet returned to the helicopter in the mid-1930s and flew a co-axial version but failed to develop it into a practical production machine. Not only was the economy against him but the French aircraft industry was being nationalized and reorganized at the time, so this added uncertainty to the equation.

The First Helicopters

It was not until the Second World War that practical production helicopters began to appear on both sides of the Atlantic. In fact, the first flew as an experimental machine in 1936. This was the Focke-Achgelis Fw 61, a twin-rotor helicopter with the rotors offset on each side of the machine and a conventional power unit and tractor propeller. This set speed and altitude records for a rotary-wing aircraft, reaching a maximum speed of

76 mph (121 kmph), reaching altitudes of up to 11,234 feet (3,424m) and remaining airborne for up to eighty minutes.

With such a performance, this had to be the precursor of a production machine, the Focke-Achgelis Fa 223 *Drache* (Dragon), powered by 1,000hp Bramo Q-3 radial engines. An initial order for 100 was issued but the first ten production machines, completed in late 1942, were all destroyed in an Allied bombing raid. Subsequent aircraft fared little better, with almost all destroyed as they came off the production line at a new factory just outside Berlin. The few that did survive were captured by the Allies as the war ended and used for trials, from which it was found that general handling of the Fa 223 was good and in some respects may have been better than the first Sikorsky machines.

A variant of the Fa 223 was the Fa 330, a rotating-wing kite designed to be towed by German U-boats while on the surface and extending their limited horizon, giving early warning of approaching surface vessels.

A competitor for the Fa 223 was the Fieseler *Storch* (Stork), a single-engined high-wing observation aircraft, which had a stall speed of just 30 mph (48 kmph) and a maximum speed of 80 mph (129 kmph).

Meanwhile, having spent most of his time since arriving in the United States, via France, from Russia, working on ever-larger amphibians and flying boats, Igor Sikorsky returned to the helicopter in 1938 when he started work on his VS-300 (Vought-Sikorsky 300). This was the classic helicopter configuration with cyclic pitch control, a single main rotor for lift and propulsion and a small tail rotor to keep the fuselage from spinning. The VS-300 was tested with Sikorsky himself at the controls in tethered flight the following year on 14 September 1939, powered by a 75hp Lycoming engine, but was not an immediate success.

The following year cyclic pitch control was abandoned and the tail rotor was supplanted by two horizontally-mounted rotors on outriggers to provide improved lateral control. A 300hp Franklin engine was used. This made a free flight on 13 May and on 6 May 1941 set a new endurance record of ninety-two minutes.

During the remainder of 1941 Sikorsky continued to refine the design, restoring partial cyclic control and removing the outriggers and their rotors before fully restoring cyclic control, installing a 150hp Franklin engine and replacing the skids with a tricycle wheeled undercarriage. While the original fuselage had been fabric-covered, it was stripped down to a bare frame for the 1940 and 1941 experiments before the fabric was restored for the final programme of test flights in 1942, which were at last successful.

The VS-300 had an open cockpit and photographs taken at the time show Sikorsky flying the helicopter while wearing a hat. This remained firmly on his head, as sitting so close to the rotor shaft there was little air movement immediately above him.

As testing continued on the VS-300, work was proceeding on the XR-4, the prototype for the R-4 series on which most of the early experiments were made.

Even while Sikorsky experimented, other designers and manufacturers continued their work. In Austria, Doblhoff experimented by using rotors with jets in the blade tips. In the USA, the Kellett Autogiro Corporation had a design using twin rotors. Nevertheless, with a few exceptions – notably the twin-rotor Vertol range of helicopters taken over by Boeing – the single main rotor and tail rotor combination has held good and has been adopted by most manufacturers.

As mentioned earlier, the United States army had been interested in helicopters since at least 1918. One organization established by the United States government between the two world wars was the National Advisory Committee for Aeronautics (NACA), which had its aeronautical laboratory at Langley Field in Virginia. It was here in 1936 that two licence-built autogiros, one built by Kellett and another by Pitcairn, were tested. The Pitcairn crashed after the canvas coating of the rotor blade ripped but the Kellett YG-1 did sufficiently well to be put into limited production. The United States Army Air Corps (USAAC) opened an auto-giro school at Patterson Field near Fairfield, Ohio, in April 1938 and ordered the YG-1.

During this period two Americans, W. Laurence LePage and Havilland H. Platt, visited Germany to look at the Focke-Achgelis Fw 61 and on returning home had designed the Platt-LePage PL-3 helicopter for the USAAC. Development was delayed until 30 June 1938, when Congress authorized the sum of US$2 million for research into rotary-wing aircraft. This sum, equal to £500,000 at the exchange rate of the day and more than £30 million by today's values, was a considerable investment at the time. On 19 July 1940, the USAAC ordered the PL-3, which it designated the XR-1 (for experimental rotary-wing 1). Not surprisingly, the XR-1 fol-lowed the configuration of the Fw 61, having an aeroplane fuselage with wingtips that had considerable anhedral (downward angle) and wingtip-mounted rotors powered by a Pratt & Whitney R-985 450hp engine. Tandem seating for two was provided and a Perspex nose allowed excel-lent forward vision.

Tethered flights started on 12 May 1941 but the XR-1 proved to be a disappointment at first. It took almost two years before the XR-1 was able to make a flight over a closed circuit and took until the end of the year before an altitude of 300 feet (91m) could be attained but this rose in 1944 to 600 feet (182m).

Given the advanced nature of the experiment, the USAAC, by now the United States Army Air Force, had decided that an alternative programme was necessary and backed Igor Sikorsky with his VS-300. In December 1940, two of Sikorsky's improved helicopter, the VS-316, were ordered and designated the Vought-Sikorsky XR-4. (It should be mentioned here that the XR-2 and XR-3 were not helicopters but improved autogiros.)

The XR-4 or VS-316 differed from the VS-300 in having just a single tail rotor after the VS-300 had been modified for trials in this form. The most noticeable difference, however, was that the machine no longer had tandem seating: the occupants sat side-by-side and were in an enclosed cabin but with a good view forward. First flown on 14 January 1942, Sikorsky's chief test pilot, Les Morris, made six flights amounting to a total of twenty-five minutes in the air with the longest flight being seven minutes, twenty seconds.

On 20 April, Morris flew the XR-4 in a demonstration for the British and American armed forces at Stratford, Connecticut. The helicopter was taken to a height of 7 feet (2.1m), hovered, then dropped back onto the take-off spot, then rose again to fly sideways, backwards, up and down and, finally, forward. A small hoop had been placed on top of an 8-foot-high (2.4m) post and the XR-4 hovered in front of it before edging forward to spear the hoop with its airspeed indicator Pitot tube, then flew to just in front of Igor Sikorsky, who took the hoop off the Pitot tube. Afterwards, the XR-4 demonstrated its ability to pick up passengers or casualties, while the VS-300 made an appearance fitted with inflated flotation bags to land on the Housatonic River and then take off again. Such a performance was nothing short of a revelation to those present.

Naturally enough, the USAAF was anxious to have the XR-4 for trials at Wright Field, Dayton, Ohio; its main experimental establishment. The easy way would have been to dismantle the rotor and transport the helicopter by road but the bold decision was taken to fly the XR-4 over the 760-mile (1,223km) route from Stratford to Dayton. However, there was still some caution in this as the direct route would have been 560 miles (901km) but a range of high mountains lay across it.

The flight began on 13 May, again with Les Morris at the controls. A car full of Sikorsky engineers accompanied the helicopter, which was hard-pressed to keep up with the car as 15 mph (24 kmph) headwinds reduced the XR-4's cruising speed from 60 mph (96 kmph) to a ground speed of 45 mph (72 kmph). Despite this, the pilots found the machine capable even in turbulence and Sikorsky himself flew for one section.

Progress was slow, with the flight being spread over five days and taking more than sixteen hours, with sixteen stops instead of the eleven originally scheduled. Nevertheless, there were no technical hitches, other than the gearbox showing occasional signs of overheating.

The trials were not confined to USAAF tests alone, as they included tests in which an XR-4 demonstrated its ability to take off from a merchant vessel with 25lb (11kg) bombs carried on the lap of the passenger and dropped onto the outline of a submarine. Later a rack was fitted to carry up to eight 25lb bombs but the surprise came as the pilots found that dropping these bombs was more accurate while flying at 40 mph (64 kmph) rather than while hovering. There were also trials using flotation gear. Before the trials ended in January 1943, an altitude record of 12,000 feet (3,658m) was reached. As a result of these trials, production started on the YR-4, the pre-production series of helicopters.

Further trials followed on the SS *Bunker Hill*, a US government-owned tanker, both with the ship lying at anchor and under way. Later a troop-ship was used with the specific intention of assessing the helicopter's suitability for anti-submarine warfare (ASW). There were also trials with the YR-4B in the Arctic, specifically for air-ambulance and liaison duties. As an air ambulance, there was insufficient room to carry patients inside, so external frames were built to carry stretchers with the patients being flown wrapped in sleeping bags.

The Royal Navy was selected to be the British service leading the trials, setting up a Helicopter Service Trials Unit with an initial 100 pilots and 150 mechanics being trained. Forty-five R-4s were supplied to the UK and most of these went to the Royal Navy with the rest passing to the Royal Air Force, which experimented with the R-4 for radar calibration work while also using it for communications duties, carrying urgent mail and despatches. In British service it was known as the Sikorsky Hoverfly and replaced the remaining Avro-built Cierva C-30 and C-40 autogiros.

Post-War Developments
Post-war, work continued on developing the helicopter, not only for military use but also for civilian purposes.

lmost certainly the wartime innovations that come to mind most often are the atomic bomb or
uclear weapons. This photograph shows examples of the first atomic bomb, known as 'Little Boy'
nd dropped on Hiroshima, with casings for the second bomb, known as 'Fat Man' and dropped on
agasaki, in the background. The two weapons used different firing mechanisms and while since
vertaken by the hydrogen or thermonuclear bomb, uranium fission remains part of the trigger
echanism for the H-bomb. (*US National Archives*)

A full-size replica of 'Fat Man',
showing the bulky casing that
required modifications to the bomb
bay of the carrier aircraft. Apart
from the differences in the
weapons, this bomb was set for a
ground-burst while the one used at
Hiroshima was detonated above
the ground. (*US National Archives*)

he need for enduring alliances was one of the factors
cognized as a result of the Second World War and this
the flag of the North Atlantic Treaty Organization,
ATO (or OTAN in French and other languages), the
ngest-lasting military treaty of all time. While the
llies eventually fought well together during the war
espite personality clashes at the top, the lack of pre-
ar alliances, exercises and collaboration ensured early
ajor defeats and the loss of much territory. (*NATO*)

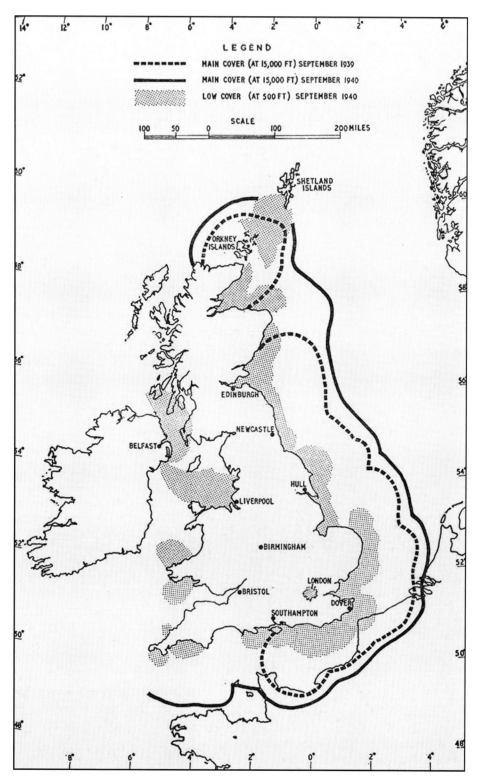

The 360ft-high (110m) transmitter towers for Chain Home at Bawdsey in Suffolk. Others such as those high up on St Boniface Down near Ventnor on the Isle of Wight received a natural boost to their height. Some also became targets but the chain was never broken. (*Imperial War Museum*)

Not only approaching enemy aircraft but also missiles pose a threat today. These are modern air defences: the radomes at Menwith Hill. (*Imperial War Museum*)

Most famous of all the air defences of the United Kingdom are those at RAF Fylingdales in Yorkshire, protecting against incoming ballistic missiles. Their presence gave rise to the so-called 'four-minute warning'. In fact, the warning was several times four minutes but the time taken to verify a threat reduced the official warning time for the civilian population to just four minutes. (*NATO*)

Earlier radar systems used scanners leaving blank spots for at least several seconds in each minute, whereas phased array radars such as this, also at RAF Fylingdales, provide a constant picture of the emerging threat. (*NATO*)

Special Forces became increasingly important during the Second World War. The British Special Air Service (SAS) can trace its origins to the Long-Range Desert Group shown here, which operated behind enemy lines in North Africa. (*Imperial War Museum*)

Bomb and land-mine disposal became an important task in British cities during the war, saving lives and avoiding much damage but at great risk to those involved. The bomb-disposal role has remained important post-war, partly because unexploded bombs and mines still appear but mainly because of terrorism, which requires bomb-disposal teams to keep abreast of developments in bomb-making. (*Imperial War Museum*)

The cruise missile can trace its origins to the German V1 flying bomb of the Second World War; the first of what Hitler termed his *Vergeltungswaffen* or 'reprisal weapons'. Unlike the latest cruise missiles that have ranges of up to 1,000 miles (1,610km), the V1 could only reach London and the south-east of England and was fired in the hope that it would hit a worthwhile target. (*German National Archive*)

The Anglo-French Storm Shadow is an air-launched cruise missile with a range of around 300 miles (483km), carrying a conventional warhead. (*MBDA*)

A much longer range comes with the US-built Tomahawk cruise missile, which can be launched from ships or from submarines and is available with conventional or nuclear warheads. (*Raytheon*)

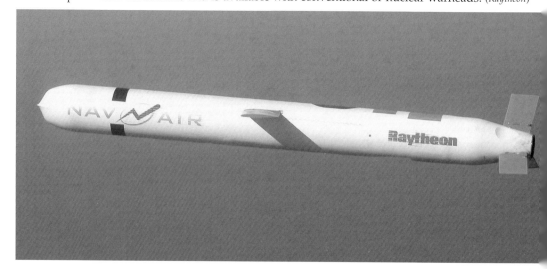

(*Above left*) The next of Hitler's *Vergeltungswaffen* was the V2, the first ballistic missile, although unlike its modern equivalents it did not leave the earth's atmosphere before plunging back to earth, had only one warhead and, like the V1, had no targeting system. It did nevertheless show the future of warfare and the possibility of space flight. A replica is shown here. (*German National Archive*)

(*Above right*) Ballistic missiles using land-based launch positions can be detected and are vulnerable, so for many years the submarine-launched ballistic missile has been used by East and West alike. The current missile for the Royal Navy and the United States navy is Trident. Here is a Trident missile launched from a submarine as it breaks from the sea. Each missile carries a number of warheads including a mix of independently-targeted nuclear warheads and decoys. (*United States Navy*)

(*Right*) As aircraft altitudes increased, anti-aircraft artillery became impotent and incapable of stopping fast high-flying bombers, so surface-to-air guided missiles (SAMs) took over. The first of these to become operational was the American Nike Ajax, shown here on a launcher. (*United States Air Force*)

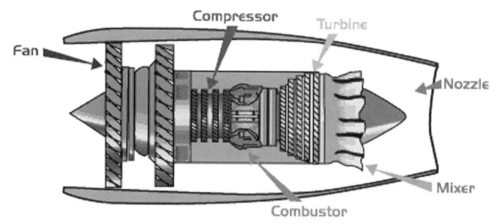

Fan

Compressor

Turbine

Nozzle

Combustor

Mixer

A cutaway drawing showing the interior of a typical turbofan engine, developed from the early turbojets of the Second World War. The first stage fan draws in the air, while the second stage compresses it before combustion and the heated air then expands so that it drives the final stage fans, powering the two earlier stages and also propelling the aircraft as it emerges at speed through the nozzle at the rear of the engine. The mixer shown before the nozzle is to reduce noise, although modern turbofans eliminate this by having a proportion of the air drawn in by the first stage turbin passed around the outside of the engine. (*NASA*)

A wartime shot of trials with the Sikorsky R-4 helicopter, with Igor Sikorsky himself sitting with his left leg out of the cockpit. The trials were mainly divided between the United States Coastguard and the Royal Navy; early on operations were conducted from ships. It did not take long for the value o the helicopter to be realized for roles such as search and rescue and liaison. (*US National Archives*)

y the early 1960s, helicopters were becoming commonplace on smaller warships such as frigates
nd destroyers. While the early small-ship helicopters were limited in their performance,
ontemporary helicopters such as the AgustaWestland Wildcat, developed from the earlier Lynx,
re fast and can carry anti-submarine torpedoes or anti-shipping missiles. (*AgustaWestland*)

he interceptor evolved during the Second World War as bomber formations began to fly at very
igh altitudes and developed during the Cold War era. The British contribution was the English
lectric, later British Aircraft Corporation (BAC), Lightning which could climb to 40,000 feet in just
ree minutes and fly at twice the speed of sound. Sadly, this splendid performance was marred by
 high accident rate and much the same was true of the Lockheed F-104 Starfighter, marketed as 'the
issile with a man in it' but known to the Luftwaffe as 'the widow-maker'. (*BAE Systems*)

The belief that precision bombing was the way forward also evolved during the war and post-war much effort was put into further developing what became known as interdiction bombing. Displaced from the strategic role by large bombers designed to carry nuclear weapons, the English Electric Canberra was one of the first to concentrate on interdiction bombing but far more sophisticated was the General Dynamics F-111 with its variable geometry mainplane, more usually known as 'swing wings'. Here an F-111 is seen dropping Mk 82 bombs. (*USAF*)

In what became an increasingly mobile war, troops were often deployed not just far from bases but also from convenient road or water transport routes, so air re-supply became important. Here is shown a Douglas C-47, known to the British as the Dakota and to the American as the Skytrain, dropping supplies over Burma. In Europe, during Operation MARKET GARDEN (the attack on Arnhem), once British troops were surrounded by the Germans, air re-supply was the only means available to keep them fighting. (*US National Archives*)

Airborne assault marked the start of the German advance in the Low Countries in 1940 and was soon adopted by the Allies. Both sides soon began building gliders capable of carrying heavy loads, including light tanks. The largest Allied glider in operational service was the Hamilcar, seen here from above with its nose doors open and a vehicle trail running away from the glider. (*Imperial War Museum*)

Search and rescue (SAR) became a highly-organized activity during the war years and while RAF Coastal Command handled long-range SAR operations, off the British coast a department within RAF Fighter Command provided airborne SAR using aircraft such as the Supermarine Walrus, seen here on trials. The RAF also had its own rescue launches at this time and for some forty years after the war ended. (*Imperial War Museum*)

Mobile warfare also required vehicles that could operate away from roads and over rough terrain. The practical solution was the Willys Jeep, a four-wheel-drive vehicle of rugged construction produced in large numbers and used by all the Allied powers. This one is clearly with US troops in the North African desert. *(US National Archives)*

Post-war, the British Rover car manufacturer, known for their luxury saloons, decided to venture into the four-wheel-drive market by producing the Land-Rover, a wider and more stable vehicle than the original Jeep. While estate car versions were later produced, the desire for something much more luxurious led to the Range Rover and what has become known as the SUV or 'sport utility vehicle'. As many of these never go off-road, they have become known in some circles as 'Chelsea Tractors', after a smart district of central London. *(Jaguar Land Rover)*

rue mobility also meant being able to travel across mixed terrain with features such as lakes and
vers. The first truly successful amphibious vehicle was the American DUKW, pronounced 'duck',
hich could be used in amphibious assaults or simply as a transport. It was also seaworthy and it is
ill possible to find civilianized DUKWs at work for offshore tourist attractions. This one is shown
·ossing the Rhine. *(Imperial War Museum)*

hile amphibious tanks were used by the Allies, much to the surprise of the Germans in
ormandy, most tanks were still landed ashore from Landing Craft, Tank (LCTs) as seen here with
British Crusader tank coming ashore. This gave the Allies the power to mount assaults on
efended coastlines on a scale never previously seen in warfare. *(Imperial War Museum)*

RFA *Mounts Bay*, a landing ship dock (LSD) currently in service with the Royal Fleet Auxiliary, that part of the Merchant Navy attached to the Royal Navy to provide fleet train operations. Such landing craft are carried internally and can be floated out when the mother ship is moored offshore. On operations, the Merchant Navy personnel aboard are outnumbered by Royal Navy personnel by more than two to one. (*BAE Systems*)

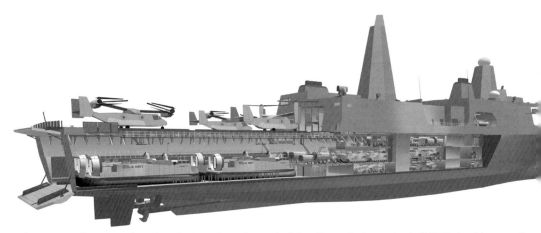

A cutaway drawing showing the interior of a typical landing platform dock (LPD); in this case the US navy's *San Antonio* class. In the USN, this is a warship along the lines of the Royal Navy's HMS *Albion* and HMS *Bulwark*. (*United States Navy*)

igates were reinvented during the Second World War by the Royal Navy, initially as ships with
uperior sea-keeping to the corvette and at first were largely specialized anti-submarine or anti-
rcraft ships. However, in the late 1950s and early 1960s the general-purpose frigate appeared as a
wer-cost alternative to the destroyer, with first helicopters and then stealth characteristics
troduced in the years that followed. This is the French *Colbert*, a modern stealth frigate with the
dar image of a fishing vessel. (*Marine Nationale*)

nderway refuelling at sea during the Second World War was slow and clumsy at first and
nerally only possible in good sea conditions with the tanker steaming ahead of the ship being
plenished. The United States navy was already using the far superior abeam method that could be
ed in a much wider range of sea conditions and this was then adopted by the Royal Navy. This is
e RFA *Fort Victoria*, one of the Royal Fleet Auxiliary's most modern ships with a 'one-stop' fuel
d stores replenishment service. (*BAE Systems*)

The Second World War saw considerable improvements in mine countermeasures, although many mines were still swept using paravanes. Today, highly-sensitive sonar capable of detecting a mine at over 3,000 feet (1,000m) is used and submersibles deployed to destroy the mine. This is a *Sandown*-class minehunter, HMS *Ramsay*. (*VT*)

A role reversal in some navies means that destroyers are now specialized while the frigate has reverted to being a general-purpose vessel. This is HMS *Daring*, one of the Royal Navy's Type 45 air-defence destroyers. (*BAE Systems*)

The first helicopter to be certified for civilian use was the Bell 47 in 1946, although once deliveries started the following year, most Bell 47s went to military customers, with licence-production by Westland in the UK, Agusta in Italy and Kawasaki in Japan. Westland was also among the licensees for the next Sikorsky helicopter, the S-51, known to the RAF and the Royal Navy as the Dragonfly and to the Americans as the R-5. Westland developed the Dragonfly with an enlarged five-person cabin, designating this variant the Widgeon. Both the Bell 47 and the Sikorsky S-51 saw service in Korea, with the Bell 47 undertaking CASEVAC (casualty evacuation) duties, while the S-51 performed plane-guard duties off aircraft carriers, rescuing naval airmen after their aircraft had ditched.

Civilian uses included the formation of the BEA Helicopter Experimental Unit by British European Airways, one of the two main predecessors of today's British Airways. Westland Dragonfly helicopters were used for experimental airmail services, while the larger Westland Whirlwind, a licence-built version of the Sikorsky S-55, was used for a number of airport feeder services, including one from Battersea in London to the capital's Heathrow Airport. These services did not prove viable but continued until withdrawal in 1956. In 1964 a subsidiary, BEA Helicopters, was formed to operate services between Penzance in Cornwall and the Isles of Scilly. This passed to another operator and was using Sikorsky S-61 helicopters when it was withdrawn in 2013. The end of this service was partly due to the high costs of operating helicopters compared to fixed-wing aircraft, a problem that was made worse by the highly seasonal nature of the route.

New York Airways was formed in 1949 and in 1952 started operating helicopters on services linking the city's airports with one another and with the centre of New York. Vertol 107 twin-rotor helicopters were used for some years before Sikorsky S-61s were introduced in 1970 but high operating costs also accounted for the demise of this service in 1979. The Vertol range of helicopters took over the twin-rotor designs pioneered in the United States by Frank Piasecki and the company was later acquired by Boeing.

In the Soviet Union considerable effort was devoted to helicopter design, starting with the small Mil Mi-1 but later a wide variety of increasingly large helicopters was built and to this day the largest helicopters built have been those of Mil, while Kamov builds small and medium-sized helicopters.

Helilift

Meanwhile, British anti-terrorist operations in Malaya saw increasing use of the helicopter. The post-war world was anything but peaceful and the

Korean War, which broke out in 1950, saw the first mass transport of troops to the battlefront by helicopter. On 20 September 1951, twelve United States navy Sikorsky S-55s lifted a company of 228 fully-equipped US marines to the top of a strategically-important 3,000-foot-high (914m) hilltop in central Korea. This was followed by the delivery of 9 tons of food and other supplies, before telegraph wires were laid back to the area headquarters. Without the use of helicopters it would have taken two days to get the troops to the top of the mountain, exposed to enemy fire all the way and with the risk of being beaten to their objective, but the helilift took just four hours.

Later, a force of 1,000 combat-equipped marines was moved to another front line in east-central Korea, taking just over six hours. By the end of January 1951, every US army and marines divisional general in Korea had at least one helicopter at his disposal for light transport and communications duties.

Equally important was the use of the helicopter for casualty evacuation. Compared with the Second World War, deaths among casualties reaching first-aid posts in Korea were down from 4.5 to 2 per cent. Not only did the helicopter shorten the time taken for casualties to reach first-aid posts, it also reduced the risk of further injuries or complications from transport over rough ground and indifferent battlefront roads.

The first heli-borne assault came in 1956 during the Anglo-French campaign to seize and secure the Suez Canal, nationalized by the Egyptians earlier that year. At dawn on 1 November, British and French carrier-borne aircraft attacked Egyptian airfields, joined by aircraft from the Royal Air Force bases in Cyprus. The initial phase of the invasion saw troops being flown ashore from the carriers in Westland Whirlwind and Bristol Sycamore helicopters, with the men lifted off the decks of the two light fleet aircraft carriers HMS *Ocean* and *Theseus*, to take Gamil Airfield near Port Said. After the successful initial assault the helicopters switched to the CASEVAC role, with one Royal Marine, wounded in fighting after landing with the first wave, arriving back aboard just twenty minutes after leaving.

The Suez operation was a political failure but a military success. It proved that it was worth building ships for the purpose of heli-borne assault and the Royal Navy was the first to recognize this, converting the light fleet carriers HMS *Albion* and *Bulwark* to commando carriers and the Fleet Air Army including two commando helicopter squadrons. Today, all major navies possess such ships, some of which have floating dock hulls.

In the wars of the late twentieth century and early twenty-first century, the helicopter proved invaluable; not only when speed was essential but also when surface transport became unsafe. In Vietnam, Northern Ireland and Afghanistan, the helicopter became the mode of transport of choice. In Vietnam, the light utility helicopter such as the Bell 205 or HU-1, later UH-1, Iroquois, capable of carrying up to fourteen troops, became the most common helicopter and many other countries bought this machine, which was also built under licence in Italy and Japan. The use of IEDs by the insurgents in Afghanistan made surface transport dangerous even in armoured vehicles and the most-used helicopter in the campaign became the Boeing CH-47 Chinook twin-rotor variant.

The use of the helicopter to carry troops is sometimes known as 'heli-lift', or in a combat zone it is sometimes described as 'vertical envelopment'. Moving supplies, especially between ships at sea, is known as 'vertical replenishment'.

By now, however, the use of the helicopter by the armies and navies of the world has broadened still further. Starting in the late 1950s, ships as small as frigates were fitted with landing platforms and hangars for helicopters that could be used for ASW. Later, even offshore patrol craft became capable of operating helicopters. Small shipboard helicopters such as the Westland Wasp were developed, using torpedoes against submarines. Larger helicopters such as the Sikorsky S-61 Sea King and its Westland equivalent, now replaced by the AgustaWestland Merlin, use dunking sonars to detect submarines. Two of the most important helicopters for ASW are the British Westland Naval Lynx, now upgraded as the Lynx Wildcat, and the American Sikorsky Sea Hawk.

Shipboard helicopters can also use air-to-surface missiles against enemy warships. Originally intended for use against missile-carrying gun boats with missiles such as the Sea Skua, larger missiles can now be carried, including the Harpoon.

Ashore, helicopters began to be equipped with anti-tank missiles and this led to the development of armed combat helicopters, such as the Bell AH-1 Cobra and the McDonnell Douglas AH-64 Apache, with the latter built under licence by AgustaWestland for the British army. The European equivalent of these is the Tiger, while the countries of the former Soviet Union and their client states use the Mil Mi-24 Hind, although this is a much larger machine with accommodation to carry a small number of troops. While the primary role of the combat helicopter, which typically has tandem seating as in a combat aircraft, is anti-tank operations, they can also fire grenades and usually have a nose-mounted heavy cannon for anti-personnel and anti-vehicle work and are also meant to be able to tackle other helicopters.

The civil uses of helicopters have also developed, largely due to the fact that much of the world's oil and natural gas supplies come from under the sea and in many parts of the world helicopters are used to ferry workers to and from the exploration and production rigs. They are also increasingly used for air-ambulance duties, especially in remote areas or in major conurbations where traffic congestion is a problem. The construction industry also uses helicopters but others use them for such work as policing, inspecting power cables and pipelines, aerial photography and filming, and even as personal transport, if you can afford it!

One weakness of the helicopter has been the need for a tail rotor in the single-rotor machines, which absorbs around 10 per cent of engine power. MDH helicopters, formerly Hughes then McDonnell Douglas Helicopters, introduced the MDH 900 Explorer, which dispenses with a tail rotor and instead uses part of the efflux from its twin turboshafts that exits by an outlet at the end of the tail and performs the same role as the tail rotor but with considerably less noise.

Vertical Take-Off

The relatively slow speed of the helicopter has led to attempts to improve airspeed, such as the compound helicopter, which has fixed wings in addition to its rotor. In the UK, Fairey designed and built the Rotodyne, using tip-mounted jets for take-off and landing while conventional turbo-props provided forward flight. This was cancelled in the late 1950s, many suggest because of noise issues. However, it was also the case that Fairey was taken over by Westland at the time, which had plans for its own large helicopter, the Westminster. More promising has been the Bell-Boeing MV-22 Osprey, which has tilting wings with turboprops placed at the outer ends driving large airscrews which perform as rotor blades for take-off and landing, then the wings transition into the horizontal for forward flight. This is in service with the US navy and USMC. That, of course, makes it a vertical take-off aircraft rather than a pure helicopter, so it is another story!

Chapter 15

Interceptors

An interceptor is a variety of fighter aircraft but while fighters should be able to engage in air-to-air combat with other fighters, the interceptor is supposed to be fast-moving, fast-climbing and able to intercept high-flying bomber aircraft. For an interceptor, speed and rate of climb are both far more important than manoeuvrability. The concept can be dated from the Second World War.

An interceptor-type aircraft was desperately needed during the First World War. Bombing could be said to date from July 1849 when Venice came under attack from the Austrians, who had been expelled the previous year. Balloons carrying 30lb (13.5kg) bombs were launched from Austrian warships offshore with a favourable wind taking them over the city; timing devices ignited the fuses but no damage was done. It was also tried on a very makeshift basis by the Italians during the Balkan Wars, largely with hand grenades tossed over the sides of aircraft.

Bombing became a serious part of strategy for both sides during the First World War. The British built the Airco DH.4 and DH.9, both effective single-engined bombers, the Handley Page 0/400 and later the Vickers Vimy; the French the Breguet 14 and 19; the Italians the Caproni Ca5; and the Germans had the Gotha Type 4, while also using Zeppelin airships on bombing raids. Yet the early fighter aircraft struggled to reach the bombers, especially the Zeppelins which could dump their water ballast and climb extremely quickly, at up to 2,000 feet (610m) in a minute. It did not help that the air defence of the United Kingdom was delegated to the RNAS, many of whose aircraft were floatplanes, and with the weight and drag of the floats, struggled to get above the airships for an attack. Attacking from below was fraught with danger for the fighters as the Zeppelin crew in their gondola under the airship could use machine-gun fire to defend themselves against the fighters.

So desperate was the situation at sea that the Royal Navy even experimented with launching landplane fighters from lighters towed at speed behind a destroyer. However, this usually meant that the fighter could only make a single sortie, having to be ditched in the sea as at the time there were no flight decks for subsequent landings.

The First World War saw bombers flying high to reach their target, hopefully out of reach of anti-aircraft fire and with enough time to spot an approaching fighter. This tactic was still in use during the Second World War, although the growing use of radar also meant that many bomber missions were flown at low level to escape detection.

The success of the bombers in the First World War was reinforced by their seeming ability to inflict destruction at will during the Spanish Civil War, so the belief became widespread among politicians and the general public that 'the bomber will always get through'. The only defence seemed at first to be maintaining a costly and manpower-intensive standing patrol of fighters at high altitude. Fortunately the growing use of radar, first seen in the British Chain Home network, gave early warning of approaching bomber formations, their direction and speed, and their altitude and numbers, allowing fighters to remain on the ground until needed. However, this then meant that the fighters had to be able to climb quickly to intercept the enemy.

Because the Supermarine Spitfire was a faster aircraft than the Hawker Hurricane, the pressing need to stop the bombers and give the Hurricane a chance to intercept them meant that during the Battle of Britain in 1940, whenever possible the Spitfire was assigned to tackling the German Messerschmitt Bf 109 fighters while the slower Hurricane took care of the bombers.

In fact the Bf 109 had much of the interceptor about it when compared with the Spitfire. It was slightly faster with a good rate of climb but less manoeuvrable. The Hurricane was the most manoeuvrable of the three, while the Spitfire was the most rugged but less easy to repair than the Hurricane. All but the earliest versions of the Bf 109 had a cannon firing through the propeller hub, which with its wing-mounted machine guns was a deadly combination that could inflict lethal damage on even the heaviest bombers.

The Germans produced the first purpose-designed interceptor in the rocket-powered Messerschmitt Me 163. This could climb quickly and reach speeds in excess of 500 mph (800 kmph) but its weakness was endurance of just eight minutes, although this could be extended by air-launch rather than from a ground-based catapult and by intermittent gliding while a target was selected.

Although the Japanese did produce rocket-powered *kamikaze* aircraft, they did not produce an interceptor. When the Boeing B-29 Superfortress appeared in the skies over Japan, Japanese fighters could not reach it unless they were stripped of their guns and ammunition, which meant that they had no option but to create *kamikaze* fighter units as well.

In the immediate post-war period, bombers continued to fly high, making it safer for them to drop nuclear weapons, and a number of interceptors were introduced by the major powers. The Soviet Union had the MiG-21; the Americans the Lockheed F-104 Starfighter, known as 'the missile with a man in it' because of its very small wings; and the British had the English Electric Lightning. A number of rocket-powered aircraft were also built and tested, including some with a so-called 'zero-length take-off' meaning that they were launched like a missile, but none achieved the success of the jet-propelled aircraft mentioned.

Air Superiority Fighters
Nevertheless, as bombers moved from high-altitude attack to low-level attack, the interceptor became less important and its place was taken by the air superiority fighter. A significant development was that the need for extended range became more important and the interceptors of the 1950s and 1960s suffered from a very short range. Interceptors could use external drop tanks to extend their range, dropping the tanks either when the fuel was exhausted or to reduce drag as they neared their target but this was only a partial solution. When being ferried from one base to another, the Lightning used over-wing tanks to extend its range. The successors became rather 'chunkier', putting on both weight and fuel.

Aircraft such as the McDonnell (later McDonnell Douglas) F-4 Phantom became more important and this was followed by the F-15 Eagle in the US and the MiG-25 in the Soviet Union and other Warsaw Pact countries, while the French had the Dassault Mirage 2000. The UK, Germany and Italy produced the Panavia Tornado IDS, a fighter variant of the multi-role aircraft that was also available as an interdictor; this used variable-geometry or 'swing-wings' to extend its range but lacked a decent operational ceiling.

Most recently, the role has passed to aircraft such as the Lockheed Martin F-16 Fighting Falcon, an American aircraft also built under licence by an alliance of European nations; the Dassault Rafale, which is also available as a carrier-borne fighter; and the Anglo-German-Italian-Spanish Eurofighter Typhoon.

Chapter 16

Interdictors

The role of the bomber is not simply to drop bombs but to attack the target and that means the right target with the right type of bomb or other air-dropped weapon.

Not only is missing the target a wasted opportunity, often conducted at great risk to the bomber and its crew, but there is also the very real danger of damaging civilian targets and killing innocent people, inflicting so-called collateral damage. One might argue that in modern warfare, civilians are often as involved as the fighting men as they produce the weapons of war but modern society has become increasingly concerned, although some might say 'jumpy', about this. In the worst-case scenario, there could be what is known as 'friendly fire' or 'blue-on-blue',* i.e. hitting one's own forces.

Bomb-aiming was at first not so much an art or a science but a game of chance; the bomb was simply dropped over the side of an aeroplane or airship. It took time for useful bomb sights to be developed and in any case, that presupposed that the aircraft actually got near the target.

Navigation was the first problem and for too long navigators were using sextants and taking sun or star readings, all designed for ships moving at 20 knots (23 mph, 37 kmph) or so, often much less, in aircraft that by 1939 were already moving at more than 200 mph (322 kmph)! To show how difficult this all was, it took no account of the weather. Low cloud or fog often obscured the target or winds drove the bomber off course, while poor meteorological practice by today's standards also meant that often too little was known about weather conditions on the way to the target or even over it. Meteorological reconnaissance became one of the war's innovations but has since been superseded by satellite observations that are continually updating.

During the Second World War, both the RAF and the Luftwaffe were forced to bomb at night whenever possible for the simple reason that this was the only way in which their losses could be kept down to a

---

*The strange term 'blue-on-blue' comes from military and naval exercises in which one's own side is 'blue' and the enemy 'red'.

sustainable level. This made accurate bombing even more difficult but the Germans used a variety of means to ensure that they got close to the target.

The Americans bombed during the day, which made navigation and bomb-aiming much easier but also required their bombers to have a heavy defensive armament, much reducing the warload that could be carried. However, to have had both the RAF and the USAAF bombing at the same time would have led to dangerous confusion and congestion in the skies around the bomber bases. Alternating day and night bombing also meant that on occasions a target could receive round-the-clock bombing, giving no time for repairs and no respite for the defenders.

Aids to Accuracy
As mentioned earlier in the chapter on radar, the first technique used by the Luftwaffe was known as *Knickebein*, transmitting radio beams from twelve ground-based stations in occupied Europe from Norway to northern France and covering the whole of the British Isles. This was an exciting development until the RAF discovered what was happening, started to jam the beams and then began to 'bend' the beams using a device known as a 'Meacon'.

In response, the Luftwaffe introduced more sophisticated techniques, still based on radio beams. These were the aforementioned *X-Gerat* and *Y-Gerat*. The former used four beams, with the first pointed at the target for navigation while the other three crossed the main beam at pre-set points in advance of the bomb-release point, enabling accurate bomb-aiming. The first of these three beams was at 31 miles (50km) from the release point; the second was at 12.5 miles (20km), at which point the observer started a special clock that acted as a stopwatch, although with two hands; the third beam was at 3 miles (5km), whereupon the observer stopped the first hand on the clock by pressing a button so that the second hand caught up with the first and when the two met, electrical contacts were closed and the bomb released automatically. The clock was a necessary part of the operation as it complemented the beams by giving accurate information about the aircraft's ground speed, otherwise strong winds could have resulted in inaccurate bombing. *Y-Gerat* used a single ground station that produced a complicated beam of 180 directional signals per minute, interpreted by equipment aboard the aircraft that re-radiated the signal back to the ground station so that the ground operators knew the exact position of the aircraft and could signal to it at the bomb-release point.

These two systems were so sophisticated that they had to use specially-trained crews who comprised the Luftwaffe equivalent of the RAF's Pathfinders and were in a special unit, *Kampfgruppe* 100, flying He 111s.

The early raids, which were inaccurate on both sides, did much to influence public opinion. A raid by the Luftwaffe intended to strike at London's docklands hit residential areas and, realizing that they could not strike at targets accurately, led the British to indulge in area-bombing rather than attempting to strike at militarily-important targets. At the beginning of the war no one would have considered such an option and in 1939 the Germans even ignored warships in Rosyth harbour for fear of hitting the adjacent town. Yet, by 1940 the Germans were happy to bomb the Dutch city of Rotterdam, even though it had been declared an 'open town', i.e. undefended. They also bombed the Channel Islands of Guernsey and Jersey after British forces had left.

In mid-December 1940, a force of 134 RAF bombers was sent to attack the German city of Mannheim and for the first time it was led by a force of Bomber Command's best crews, dropping incendiary bombs to mark the target for the main force. Of the 134 aircraft, the crews of 102 claimed to have dropped their bombs on the target but post-raid photographic reconnaissance showed that little damage had been done. In fact, in 1941 RAF Bomber Command had managed to drop just 20 per cent of its bombs within 5 miles (8km) of the target.

As previously described, various systems were introduced to improve RAF bombing accuracy. The first of these was GEE (as in 'G' for grid), with signals from ground stations guiding the bomber towards its target. The navigator aboard the aircraft had a chart with the GEE grid over-printed and the ground stations' signals were picked up and displayed on a cathode ray tube. Signals from three stations were used to obtain the bomber's position within an accuracy of between half a mile (0.8km) and 5 miles (8km) over distances of 300 to 400 miles (483 to 644km), which meant that British bombers could reach Germany's most dense industrial area, the Ruhr. It was realized that Bomber Command had at most six months from the introduction of GEE early in 1942 before the Germans managed to jam or bend the radio beams. In fact in one raid on Essen, with the target marked by incendiaries, the Germans managed to lay false flares so that the bomb-aimers dropped their bombs in the wrong places.

An inquiry was set up to investigate Bomber Command's accuracy. Many believed that the answer lay in an elite force for target-finding and marking. This eventually resulted in the creation of the Pathfinder Force, although this was at one time opposed by those who objected to the selection of units as being in any way special.

In the meantime, other aids were introduced to improve accuracy. The first of these was OBOE, which took radio beams from two ground stations with one being the 'cat'. The 'cat' station provided a circular route so that the bomber was always at a constant range from the ground station's audible signal. The other station was the 'mouse', giving the signal for the aircraft to bomb the target. This equipment was not ready for service until late 1942. One problem was that as the aircraft flew further from the ground station, it had to climb because of the earth's curvature and over the Ruhr this meant flying at 28,000 feet (8,534m), beyond the capabilities of any bomber with a decent warload at the time. Another problem was that the 'cat' and 'mouse' system could only control one bomber at a time.

Far better was H2S, a downward-pointing rotating radar transmitter that scanned the ground over which the aircraft was flying, with changes in terrain being detectable on a cathode ray tube. This meant that the navigator could detect the change from open country to a built-up area but it was most effective when there was an even sharper contrast, as occurred between water and a built-up area such as docks, for example. A specially-trained operator could use H2S both for navigation and for bomb-aiming. The technique had been identified as early as 1937 but was overlooked while priority was given to defensive radars. The system had a range of up to 40 miles (64km) but it had one weakness: it could be detected by the Germans, making interception of the bombers by night-fighters much easier. When finally developed, the system had been intended for RAF Coastal Command and there then followed an internal wrangle between leaders of the two commands over who should be given priority in the allocation of the H2S sets.

By 1943, with H2S and OBOE, the RAF was getting 70 per cent of its bombs within 3 miles (5km) of the target.

One of the first precision raids, and one of the most famous bombing raids of the Second World War, was the RAF's attack on the Ruhr Dams on the night of 16/17 May 1943, code-named Operation CHASTISE.

The idea was to use mines, more usually known to the public as 'bouncing bombs', against three dams standing in the Ruhr Valley – the Möhne, the Eder and the Sorpe – with the intention of damaging German electricity generation. Paradoxically, the dams were not as important for this as the British had thought as most of Germany's electricity generation was from coal-fired power stations; however, the resultant shortage of water did inflict considerable problems on the steel industry and also on the coking plants for gas production.

A special squadron, No. 617, was formed in spring 1943 with some of Bomber Command's leading pilots, navigators and bomb-aimers. The idea was to send twenty aircraft against the dams using a special mine, known as 'Upkeep', which was designed to bounce before settling against the base of the dam well below the water level. It was important not only to reach the dams but to drop the mines at a specific height above the water if they were to have any chance of success. To achieve this, spotlights were fitted to the nose and tail of each bomber and angled so that the beams crossed at a specific point which, when reflected on the surface of the water, meant that the aircraft was exactly 60 feet (18.3m) above the water. The raid was scheduled for the night of 16/17 May 1943 when the water level at the dams was expected to be at its highest.

Of the 19 aircraft sent, only 12 reached the target with 5 being lost and 2 turning back, one because it lost its bomb when it flew too close to the sea on the outbound flight and the other because of anti-aircraft fire damaging the intercom.

No. 617 Squadron managed to breach two of the dams, the Möhne and the Eder, as required. The Sorpe was also breached, with a second mine widening the initial breach; however, the damage was slight as only the top part of the structure was affected. During the raid the squadron's commanding officer, Wing Commander Guy Gibson, made the first run, dropping his mine at the Möhne Dam, and for the rest of the operation he took on the role of what later became known as the 'master bomber', providing advice and guidance to the other bomber pilots. He also used his aircraft to draw flak away from the others while they made their attacks. This meant hanging around and circling while the other pilots made their bombing runs, which was extremely dangerous and earned him the VC (Victoria Cross) for valour.

A little over two months later, Operation GOMORRAH, the bombing of Hamburg, started on the night of 24/25 July. This was a target well-suited to the use of H2S as the city was on the coast. While it was of immense strategic value, it is hard to suggest that this was true interdiction bombing as it was a mass bombing raid, noteworthy for the first use of 'window' (dropping aluminium foil strips to confuse enemy radar) and the aircraft massed together so that the enemy could get little idea of their numbers. A total of 791 heavy bombers were used, of which 728 reached the target with 40 per cent of the bombs landing within 3 miles (5km) of the city centre. The following night, 705 aircraft were sent against Essen with 604 reaching the city and 60 per cent of the bombs landing within the target area.

Bomber missions with specific objectives such as oil refineries and rubber or ball-bearing plants were regarded as vital by the Americans. Air Chief Marshal Sir Arthur 'Bomber' Harris, head of RAF Bomber Command, dismissed these as 'panacea targets' but depriving the Axis war machine of fuel or the essential components for manufacturing aircraft and vehicles was surely the way forward. One problem was, of course, the distance of some of these targets from air bases in England, mainly in the east of the country. To avoid this, some USAAF operations were mounted from bases in Libya. For example, bombing the oil plants at Ploesti in Romania was carried out during the day, as were most US bombing missions, and required 9 tons of fuel for the 2,100-mile round trip, so the warload of each aircraft was just 2 tons. Unfortunately the first raid on Ploesti suffered from a number of errors, with some of the bombers heading for Bucharest before they realized their mistake and turned back towards Ploesti, while others approached from the wrong direction. Worst of all, thanks to German code-breakers, the Germans and the Romanians knew they were coming.

More in line with the concept of interdiction bombing was the raid on the V-weapons research establishment at Peenemünde, Operation HYDRA, on 17/18 August 1943. The British had been aware that the Germans were experimenting with rockets since November 1939 but at first many had dismissed this as either German propaganda or a German false trail. It was not for another two years that the reports began to be taken seriously.

For accuracy at Peenemünde, several techniques were used. Mosquito pathfinders laid incendiaries to mark the target, while there was also a master bomber, as on Operation CHASTISE (the 'Dambusters' raid). Offset marking was used as well. This entailed setting markers at a distance from the target, especially useful if the target area was obscured by low cloud. A fourth technique was 'time and distance' marking, with yellow incendiaries laid preceding red and green incendiaries at the target. As even this combination had not always guaranteed complete accuracy, 'Bomber' Harris also opted for a moonlit night, even though this would also make it easier for German fighters to spot the bombers.

The target was regarded as so vital that no fewer than 596 aircraft were directed towards it, led by 16 Pathfinders. H2S was used for pathfinding but it failed to work as well as expected because, despite Peenemünde being on the coast, because of swampy ground nearby, the red markers were dropped south of their intended location. The first wave of Short Stirlings bombed the wrong target but Group Captain John Searby, who was leading the raid and acting as master bomber, realized this, helped by a force of Pathfinders that had been held in reserve. Searby was also able to intervene when two further groups of bombers were in danger of being misled after the wind direction had changed and started to drive the target incendiaries out to sea. Unfortunately, he did not notice that the markers on the third aiming-point had not been placed correctly.

Despite these problems, considerable damage was done and production of the V2 rocket was delayed by the 3.5 million pounds of high explosive and almost 600,000 pounds of incendiaries. Anti-aircraft fire over the target was much less than expected and many German night-fighters had been drawn away by a diversionary raid on Berlin. Nevertheless, almost forty aircraft were lost in the attack.

Fighting the Gestapo

Before this an operation had already been conducted that had all the marks of interdiction bombing showing incredible precision. On 25 September 1942, the Germans in Norway had planned a rally of their collaborators. British intelligence had become aware of this and so an attack on the Gestapo (German secret police) headquarters in Oslo was planned as a morale booster for the Norwegian people. This operation would require pinpoint accuracy and was carried out by four de Havilland Mosquito bombers of No. 105 Squadron, led by Squadron Leader George Parry.

To escape detection by enemy radar, the four aircraft had to cross the North Sea at an altitude of less than 100 feet (30m) and use dead reckoning for navigation, despite the long distance of more than 500 miles (805km) each way. Each aircraft carried four 500lb bombs with eleven-second delayed-action fuses so that the aircraft would not be blown up by their own bombs as they dropped. Despite the low altitude, the aircraft were pounced on by two Focke-Wulf Fw 190 fighters, forcing one of the attackers to make a forced landing in the Oslofjord, while in attempting to escape from the fighters, another aircraft clipped a tree and had to break off the attack.

This left just two aircraft with a total of eight bombs to press home the attack, which was less successful than intended as of the four bombs that struck the building, one failed to explode and the other three careered through the building and out of a wall before exploding. The Gestapo headquarters was not destroyed but nearby houses were and eighty

Norwegian civilians were killed or wounded. Despite this, the raid was used to unveil the Mosquito to the British public for the first time.

More successful was the attack on Amiens Prison in France on 18 February 1944. The prison held around 700 French captives, of whom 250 were political or resistance prisoners. The idea was to knock down the walls of the prison so that the prisoners could escape so, for obvious reasons, this was known as Operation JERICHO. It was requested by the head of a French Resistance group because not only were mass executions imminent but there was also concern that under torture some of the prisoners might have given a clue to Allied plans for landings in France, although these had yet to be finalized by the Allies themselves at this stage.

Three RAF squadrons of No. 140 Wing each contributed six aircraft to the operation, resulting in a combined Anglo-Australian-New Zealand mission. Three squadrons of Hawker Typhoons were to provide an escort. To ensure that the bombs did not fly over the prison wall and hit the main building, the attack had to be made with the aircraft flying at between 10 and 15 feet (3 and 4.5m) above the ground. Three aircraft were to attack one corner and another three the corner diagonally opposite, with another four aircraft held in reserve. A further three had to attack the annexe housing the prison warders and another six the annexe at the other side of the prison housing the Gestapo. Finally, six aircraft were held in reserve in case any of the earlier flights failed in their objectives.

The first wave of aircraft was timed to attack at 12:03, with the second wave attacking at 12:06. The aircraft from the RAF squadron were to hold off until 12:16 and to return with their bombs if the preceding attacks had been successful. Two additional aircraft were present: one filming the raid and the other carrying the wing's commanding officer, who was in effect the master bomber.

Bad weather with heavy snow and low cloud delayed the mission, so by the time it was launched, time was running short. The poor weather continued, so that only eight out of the twelve Typhoons assigned to cover the operation managed to make the rendezvous. Snow was covering the ground, making the identification of landmarks difficult, and by the time they reached the gaol, the first formation of six aircraft was down to five, with the second down to just four. Nevertheless, the walls were breached and the two annexes destroyed. One bomb overshot and hit the roof of the main building but this had the beneficial effect of shattering the bolts and locks on cell doors so that the prisoners had just to push them open.

Nevertheless, scores of prisoners died in the attack with many others wounded. Resistance forces swarmed into the prison after the walls were breached and 400 prisoners escaped, with all clear by 12:15. A number were soon recaptured or gave themselves up but among the 250 who remained free, 12 had been due to be shot the following day. The attack killed 102 prisoners and around 50 guards, while 74 prisoners were wounded, many by small-arms fire from the guards. Some prisoners remained to help the wounded, including some guards and Gestapo members, and some of these were pardoned by the Germans.

As the attackers flew back, the wing commander's aircraft was caught by a lone Fw 190 which shot off its tail and caused it to dive out of control, killing both the crew.

Other operations against Gestapo buildings followed. A successful raid on Aarhus in October 1944 was followed by one on Copenhagen on 21 March 1945, requested by the Danish resistance and code-named Operation CARTHAGE. The latter destroyed the Gestapo headquarters but one of the aircraft clipped a lamppost with its wing and crashed into a school, killing 86 schoolchildren and 18 adults, many of them nuns teaching in the school. Losses also included 55 Germans, 47 of their Danish civilian employees and 8 prisoners. Several of the Mosquitos and their North American Mustang fighter escorts were lost. An attack on Gestapo headquarters in The Hague was successful and was timed to occur while children in the adjacent school were away for lunch.

Post-War Developments
Post-war, the concept of interdiction bombing was not ignored but increasing attention was paid to the use of nuclear and then thermo-nuclear weapons. However, as the RAF's V-bombers arrived for this role, the service's English Electric Canberra jet bombers were assigned to interdiction.

Interdiction bombing was used in the Korean War in the early 1950s, mainly by carrier-borne aircraft against targets including bridges as the number of hard targets in mainly rural Korea was extremely limited.

Few further opportunities for interdiction occurred until the start of the Vietnam War, which lasted from 1955 to 1975. As in Korea, the number of suitable targets was limited and again, bridges seemed to be one of the major opportunities. Losses among USN and USAF aircraft were relatively high with the North Vietnamese launching surface-to-air missiles in salvoes but a change came both in the number of aircraft lost and the accuracy of the strikes with the growing use of stand-off weapons.

The Western intervention to liberate Kuwait and then against Iraq a few years later saw a marked change, with interdiction bombing replaced by the use of cruise missiles providing growing accuracy against important targets.

It is hard to avoid the conclusion that the days of pure interdiction bombing may have passed and that the future relies on using either stand-off weapons or cruise missiles to attack key targets with pinpoint accuracy. This may seem far less exciting but the use of stand-off weapons or cruise missiles has made warfare much safer for the attacker. An innovation in the conflict in Afghanistan has been the use of armed drones, more properly known as unmanned aerial vehicles (UAVs), to seek out and destroy key targets, including the leaders of terrorist groups. The UAVs have been criticized for causing the deaths of non-combatants but as will have been noticed, this was often a hazard of interdiction bombing.

Chapter 17

Air Re-supply

Using aircraft to support ground forces with supplies and reinforcements really dates from the 1920s when the Royal Air Force used bomber-transports in Mesopotamia against warring tribesmen. The aircraft at the time were dual-role and could be used either as bombers or as transports and by the standards of later years were not particularly efficient in either role. By the outbreak of the Second World War, the concept of the bomber-transport was outdated and gone, even though the mainstay of the Luftwaffe's transport fleet was the Junkers Ju 52/3m trimotor that had first emerged as a bomber-transport and had been used as such during the German intervention in the Spanish Civil War.

The bomber-transport category does not include those German aircraft of the 1930s such as the Dornier Do 17 that were officially designed as transports – airliners in fact – but had largely entered production as bombers. These were cramped and uncomfortable as airliners but clearly intended to be bombers. By this time the design of bombers and airliners had diverged considerably, as proved by many post-war conversions of bombers, such as the Avro Lancaster into the Lancastrian airliner, with their fuselage too cramped for comfort.

Despite the great distances and poor roads, air re-supply was not used extensively during the North African campaign. There was some use of it during the Siege of Malta between 1940 and 1943, with Imperial Airways flying desperately-needed supplies to the island from Gibraltar under cover of darkness. However, there were three great instances of air re-supply being used during the Second World War. The first of these was from India to British and Indian forces in Burma and to Chinese Nationalist Forces; the second was at Arnhem during Operation MARKET GARDEN, when forces relieving the airborne troops who had landed to seize the bridge over the Rhine were delayed; and the third was when German forces were encircled by Soviet troops at Kursk.

The war years saw vast improvements in the quality and efficiency of transport aircraft. In fact, one of the most successful of the transport aircraft available was the Douglas C-47, known to the British as the Dakota and to the Americans as the Skytrain. This was a late pre-war development as the DC-3 (Douglas Commercial 3), the latest in a family of airliners that had started with the DC-1 and been followed by the DC-2, but it was the DC-3 that became one of the outstanding airliners of all time. There was also a larger aircraft, the Curtiss C-46. Most British aircraft production during the war years concentrated on combat aircraft but one exception was the Avro York. This used the same wing and tailplane design as the Lancaster bomber but had a fuselage that was definitely proportioned to make an effective transport.

Gliders were used extensively, both by the Allies and the Germans. There were a number of reasons for this. The gliders themselves were simple, much easier and cheaper to build than powered aircraft, needed less maintenance and could be flown by pilots with less lengthy and expensive training than that required by pilots of powered aircraft. They would also be towed into position by heavy bombers, so these aircraft could be useful in more than just their combat role. A couple of glider designs were also built as powered versions, having inspired aircraft designers by their capacity.

Air re-supply was not an easy option, much less a safe one. It helped if a landing strip was available but the aircraft were then vulnerable on the ground. On the Eastern Front and at Arnhem, supplies often landed among the enemy, while in Burma much of it landed in the jungle. Trying to get supplies landed in the right area meant flying steadily through intense anti-aircraft fire, so flying a transport was not a soft option. The aircraft of the day still had their limitations regarding speed and payload. There was nothing to compare with the 50-ton capacity of a Boeing C-17 Globemaster III or the 15 to 20 tons of a Lockheed Martin C-130 Hercules.

Air re-supply is clearly different from airborne assault, as with the German invasion of The Netherlands in May 1940, the Allied assaults in Sicily and the Normandy landings, or even the transport of troops of the Spanish Foreign Legion from North Africa in 1936 by General Franco at the start of the Spanish Civil War.

The USAAF had an Air Transport Command (ATC) that had emerged in 1942 from the US Air Corps Ferrying Command established in 1941. At its wartime peak, the USAAF ATC had 200,000 personnel and 3,700 aircraft. The RAF also created a Transport Command to sit alongside its combat commands and this was established in 1943.

Over the 'Hump'
As the Japanese advanced through China in December 1941, they cut off an American volunteer group fighting alongside the Chinese Nationalist

Forces. The Americans had been in China since September, flying Curtiss P-40 Warhawk fighters, and the Japanese advance meant either curtailing operations or being supplied by air. Fortunately, by this time the United States had officially entered the war as a result of the Japanese attack on the US Pacific Fleet at Pearl Harbor. Prior to this, the US government had had to deny any knowledge of the volunteer group.

The problem was that any supplies would have to be flown over part of the Himalayas that rose to 16,000 feet (4,877m) along the route to be taken, later known to air-crews as the 'hump'. An easier and more direct route was available to the volunteer base at Kunming but this was exposed to attack by Japanese fighter aircraft. Initially Douglas C-47s were used, with each aircraft carrying about 2.5 tons of supplies. The service started early in 1942, using an improvised network of bases established in north-east India, which was supplied by railways from a major depot in Calcutta.

The squadrons used in carrying supplies to China were incorporated in the USAAF ATC when it was established in December 1942, by which time the volunteer group had become part of the official United States China Task Force.

The supplies carried by air rose steadily from 2,800 tons to 7,000 tons a month by the end of 1943 and during 1944 this rose further to 12,000 tons a month. This growth in monthly tonnage was made possible by the addition of the larger Curtiss C-46 Commandos on the airlift while a number of the four-engined Douglas C-54 Skymaster, the military variant of the DC-4 airliner, were also made available. The inevitable dispute arose between the military commanders and airmen over who should take priority for the supplies. This was resolved by the commander-in-chief of the India-Burma-China theatre, Lieutenant General Joseph 'Vinegar Joe' Stilwell, who allocated the supplies 50:50 between ground and air forces.

The airlift over the hump was not confined to carrying supplies, as in April 1944 it also carried 18,000 Chinese troops to India to participate in Stilwell's advance during the Burma campaign.

Behind Enemy Lines

Meanwhile, starting in 1943, British forces were operating behind Japanese lines in Burma; an operation that was only possible because of the availability of transport aircraft and gliders. This was the idea of Colonel, later Major General, Orde Wingate: a soldier rather than an airman but rightly described by his commanding officer General, later Field Marshal, Wavell as a 'genius for novel and unorthodox warfare'. Wingate's force was officially known as the Long-Range Penetration Brigade but was usually known as the 'Chindits', a corruption of the Burmese word for 'winged stone lion', the guardians of Buddhist temples.

Wingate's force initially comprised 3,000 men, organized into eight columns, each of which had an RAF liaison officer. The force penetrated Japanese-held territory on foot but were kept supplied by Douglas C-47 Dakotas of No. 31 Squadron and Lockheed Hudsons of No. 194 Squadron, Royal Air Force. The following year another 2,000 troops were flown in, while 10,000 were either air-landed by glider or parachuted in to reinforce the Chindits. The reinforcements were necessary so that the Chindits could capture and dominate the Indaw-Kaha area and, having secured the ground, hold it until relieved by Stilwell's advancing troops. For this, air support was on a more generous scale, with support from the USAAF providing no fewer than seven squadrons of C-47s as well as combat and liaison aircraft.

Dropping supplies over the jungle was no easy task and required good airmanship. The Chindits cut drop zones that were narrow and no more than 60 yards (55m) in length. The first drop was largely a failure but lessons were quickly learned as any supplies that missed the drop zones were lost in the jungle. Four Waco CG-4A gliders brought bridging equipment so that a bridge could be built over the Chindwin River by 4 March 1944. Airstrips were also built and given code names, such as 'Broadway', 'Piccadilly' and 'Chowringhee', later joined by 'Aberdeen'.

No fewer than twenty-six C-47s each towed two CG-4A gliders, keeping to a minimum altitude of 8,000 feet (2,438m) and after releasing the gliders, the C-47s had to climb to 9,000 feet (2,743m) to clear the mountains surrounding the landing zones. A later fleet of eighty gliders was allocated equally to 'Broadway' and 'Piccadilly' but a reconnaissance flight showed that the Japanese had blocked 'Piccadilly' by felling trees across the strip. The decision was taken to reduce the number of gliders to sixty, all of which would land at 'Broadway', with the first eight sent ahead carrying engineers who could clear the strip if the Japanese had blocked it. One cannot help but wonder how they would have landed if that had been the case!

As if flying over mountains and dense jungle to land at a very basic landing strip was not bad enough, this operation was to be conducted at night. To achieve this the towing aircraft had to fly as low as possible along a line of lights, oil-fired flares, with the glider pilots cutting their tows at a point half a mile from the landing strip, marked by another flare.

On landing, the gliders, which had retained their undercarriages instead of dropping them after take-off, would roll clear of the landing strip.

The eight gliders carrying the advance party of engineers landed successfully, as did the first two gliders of the main wave, but the three pairs that followed all encountered a ditch on the landing strip which knocked off their undercarriages and sent them spinning around, blocking the strip. Before the flares could be realigned to guide the following gliders around the wreckage, several more landed on the wreckage, killing two men and injuring several others. Fortunately, another two spotted the wreckage in the poor light and managed to glide over it.

A message was sent cancelling a follow-up airlift of heavy equipment but only eight of nine gliders, all being towed singly, returned while one continued. This glider landed too fast and while it sailed over the earlier wreckage, could not stop on what remained of the airstrip. It crashed into the jungle at the end of the strip but while the glider was brought to a stop, the bulldozer it was carrying surged forward. However, as it did so it raised the nose of the glider with the two pilots sitting in it so that they survived the accident while the bulldozer was wrecked in the jungle.

The airstrip was cleared by dawn and 400 troops put in position to guard it while it was lengthened and widened so that night troops could be flown in aboard C-47s. The first landing was by an aircraft carrying just 4,500lbs (2,041kg) but this was so successful, despite landing in the wrong direction, that later landings carried 6,000lbs (2,722kg). 'Chowringhee' was also improved but there was some doubt as to whether it really was suitable for transport aircraft and a message was sent cancelling the first twenty aircraft; however, seven did not receive the message and landed successfully. Nevertheless, 'Chowringhee' was too close to the Japanese for safety, being only 15 miles (24km) from a good road, and it was decided to abandon it. Two hours after the Chindits and the last aircraft had left, it was attacked by Japanese fighter-bombers.

The variety of cargo and passengers carried during the air re-supply operation was considerable. Aircraft were adapted to carry mules, while the passengers included native Burmese tribesmen who had sided with the Allies.

Inevitably, there were wounded men to be flown out of the operational zone. Some had been moved by the liaison aircraft but these were too small, so it was decided to evacuate most of them by glider. This required two lightweight poles to be erected with the glider's tow line passed between them, while the C-47 tug would fly with a hook mounted under the fuselage. As the hook on the tug aircraft caught the glider's tow line, the poles collapsed, the C-47 boosted its engine power to take the strain of the glider and the glider was snatched into the air.

This was a very difficult operation and it had to be first trialled in the United States. The pilots of the C-47 and the gliders needed considerable skill but it worked most of the time. Surprisingly, the consensus among the C-47 pilots was that it took less engine power to snatch a glider off the ground than for a normal towed take-off from a runway, possibly because the towing aircraft was already in the air.

In late March 1944, a patrol landed behind Japanese lines in five gliders, carried out an operation to disrupt Japanese supplies and was then snatched away using the same five gliders.

The Chindits tied down four Japanese divisions, a far larger force than theirs. The third and final phase of their campaign involved the last of the airstrips, 'Aberdeen', constructed by glider-landed US army engineers. Work began on the night of 22 March 1944 and took just two days. From the start, 'Aberdeen' was able to handle C-47 transports but the original plan to operate sixty C-47 sorties a night over six nights to airlift two brigades into 'Aberdeen' was unachievable because the air transport force was under intense pressure as the Allies faced a major Japanese counter-attack. So instead only ten sorties a night could be flown and it took more than twenty nights from 23 March to airlift the two brigades into 'Aberdeen'.

In the meantime, Indian troops blocked the main Japanese supply lines at a point code-named 'White City'. A landing strip was cleared at 'White City' and despite being waterlogged by heavy rain on the first night, 5 April, 26 C-47s landed under the cover of darkness controlled by an Aldis lamp and discharged more than 250 men, 4 25-pounder guns, 6 Bofors guns and a number of anti-tank weapons.

The Chindits were engaged in highly mobile warfare, so many of the original landing strips were closed and fresh ones opened. One of the new bases was on the shores of Lake Indawgyi and was named 'Blackpool'. This was supplied by two Royal Air Force Short Sunderland flying boats and on 25 May 1945 these aircraft also evacuated casualties.

Meanwhile, 'Aberdeen' had one of the first wartime missions for the helicopter. Shortly after the base was opened, Lieutenant Carter Harman of the USAAF flew one of the frail Sikorsky R-4 machines on a 130-mile (209km) flight from a forward air base over a 5,000-feet-high (1,524m) mountain range. This flight was only possible with auxiliary fuel tanks which were positioned above the pilot's head. While at 'Aberdeen', the helicopter rescued three wounded British soldiers and a downed fighter pilot, flying them out one at a time from a paddy field.

Given the success of the air transport support for the Chindits, it was especially sad that the architect of the operation, Orde Wingate, was killed on 24 March 1944 when the North American B-25 Mitchell bomber in which he was travelling crashed and exploded while landing.

MARKET GARDEN

Back in Europe, the Allied invasion of Sicily and the Normandy landings had both been supported by paratroops and glider-landed forces, taking their cue from the German use of airborne troops earlier in the war.

A completely different plan was Operation MARKET GARDEN, the code name for the airborne assault on Arnhem in The Netherlands on 17 September 1944. In fact, the action comprised two operations: MARKET to seize the bridges over the Maas and Waal and the lower Rhine; and GARDEN, the approach of British XXX Corps over the ground. The idea was that leap-frogging over German positions, holding strategic objectives and waiting for advancing ground troops to join up with the airborne troops, would hasten the Allied advance and shorten the war. A great deal of hope was invested in this operation, with some believing that it could help towards ending the war before the end of 1944. Unfortunately, because of heavy German anti-aircraft defences around the bridges, the British paratroops had to be landed so far from their objectives that any element of surprise was lost, while Dutch resistance reports of two German *Panzer* divisions refitting nearby were discounted by the Allies. The American paratroops fared much better, except that one of their bridges was destroyed by the Germans before they could reach it.

The Arnhem operation was one of the largest airborne assaults of the Second World War with more than 2,000 gliders, tugs and troop-carrying aircraft involved. However, all did not go well, with the British losing two of their large Hamilcar gliders which nosed into soft soil and overturned, damaging the invaluable anti-tank guns carried aboard, while among the thirty-five gliders that failed to land on the current landing zones were those carrying armoured jeeps intended to get the British paratroops quickly to their objectives. Rather than taking the bridge over the Rhine, the British arrived to find themselves confronted by German troops on the bridge itself.

Not least of the problems facing the British was that General Kurt Student, the German paratroops commander, was in the area at the time and there was no one better able to assess and predict what the Allies were planning, while the German commander at Nijmegen, General Walter Model, was quick to respond.

The real problem for the British forces once on the ground was the failure of the air re-supply operation. This was crucial, especially as the advance of XXX Corps took far longer than anticipated. A combination of factors was behind the failure, including heavy anti-aircraft fire, bad weather and the ever-tightening German encirclement of the British troops, which meant that just 7 per cent of the supplies dropped reached the British. It was difficult to reset markers showing the extent of the British area as the German grip tightened.

Among the crews of the re-supply aircraft there was no shortage of bravery as they attempted to fly a straight and steady course through heavy anti-aircraft fire. On the first day of the re-supply operation, 19 September, 100 aircraft were allocated from the RAF's No. 38 Group and another 63 from No. 46 Group; 13 aircraft were lost and a further 97 seriously damaged. Over the next two days, 38 Group suffered almost 200 casualties among its air-crew. By 21 September the operation was ending, with the Rhine bridge having been held for the planned three-and-a-half days. In the days that followed, British, Polish and American troops fought to join the advancing troops but out of 10,000 British and Polish troops, just 3,000 returned with the rest either killed or taken prisoner by the Germans.

Fortunately, far greater success awaited the Allies the following year in Operation VARSITY, the crossing of the Rhine.

Struggling to Survive in the East

Meanwhile the Germans, who had been the leaders in airborne assault, were not having the same success with air re-supply. Part of the problem was that they did not have a dedicated air transport command and instead used instructors from the bomber-pilot training schools whenever an airborne assault was needed. Therefore air re-supply was not an option readily chosen by the Germans; instead a necessity that had to be forced upon them.

The first theatre of war where air re-supply became a necessity was North Africa. Using Malta as a base, British air and naval action in the Mediterranean substantially reduced the flow of supplies from Italy to the German *Afrika Korps*, even though Malta's very survival was threatened by the Axis powers that had themselves been effective in closing the Mediterranean to British merchant shipping. As early as September 1941, the flow of supplies to North Africa had been cut by 40 per cent.

A year later the situation had become so bad, despite the misuse of hospital ships by the Italians to carry supplies, that the Luftwaffe and the Italian *Regia Aeronautica* were forced to provide an air-bridge across the Mediterranean. Inevitably, Allied fighter aircraft were soon on the scene and in November 1942 the Luftwaffe alone lost seventy Junkers Ju 52/3m transports. In December, twenty of the giant six-engined Messerschmitt Me 323 *Gigant* transports, as well as large numbers of gliders, joined the air-bridge; a sign of the increasing desperation of the Axis forces. The Me 323 was itself a development of the Me 321 glider, which was so big that it needed three tug aircraft to get it into the air. Other aircraft included the Junkers Ju 90 and 290, and the Focke-Wulf Fw 200 which with 400 Ju 52/3m managed to lift 9,000 men and almost 5,000 tons of supplies and equipment in December 1942 and again in January 1943. The Me 323 was used mainly for carrying heavier and bulkier items, while the main cargo for the other aircraft was fuel.

This was clearly not an effort on the scale of that provided by the USAAF and RAF in the Far East. Despite the introduction of larger, faster and more modern aircraft, the Luftwaffe's transport effort throughout the war relied heavily on the obsolete Ju 52/3m, dated even before the war began. The Ju 900 and Fw 200 were really maritime-reconnaissance aircraft, suggesting that perhaps these had been pulled away from other duties.

Another case of the Germans being forced to use air re-supply because nothing else was available came in the retreat from Moscow.

The Germans had been late in launching the invasion of the Soviet Union, Operation BARBAROSSA. There were several reasons for this. One was the fact that they had had to intervene in the Balkans to rescue their Italian allies whose advances into Yugoslavia and Greece had become hopelessly bogged down. Another was that heavy spring rains had left the ground too soft for heavy vehicles such as tanks. The invasion had also been hampered by Hitler's insistence that the German forces should wheel south and north to capture the Ukraine and Leningrad to secure raw materials and seize industrial plant rather than head straight for Moscow. This gave the forces around Moscow time to reorganize and prepare for a fresh counter-attack.

Worse still, not only had the Germans underestimated the fighting prowess of the Soviet forces and their ability to replace lost matériel through a system of shadow factories east of the Urals and outside the range of German bombers, but the Germans themselves were very ill-equipped for fighting once the Russian winter came.

The first winter after the invasion, that of 1941–2, was bitterly cold with heavy snow. Retreating from Moscow under heavy Soviet attack, the German 2nd Corps was surrounded at Demyansk in February 1942. The Germans, who had seemed unstoppable in 1940, had 100,000 troops cut off. Hitler overruled his generals, forbade an attempted break-out to the rear and demanded that the Luftwaffe supply the troops. Hermann Göring, the Luftwaffe's commander-in-chief, was in no position to argue as his position was weak after failing to break the Royal Air Force in the Battle of Britain and having been unable to stop British air-raids on Germany.

For the first and only time, the Luftwaffe's air supply operation succeeded. However, success was bought dearly, requiring no fewer than 160 trainloads of aviation fuel and no less than 262 Ju 52/3m transports and many of their brave crews. A senior officer had been given responsibility for air transport the previous October, but not senior enough to challenge proposals for an air supply operation in unsuitable conditions. Yet, from this time onwards Hitler consistently refused to sanction retreats or even withdrawals that might have strengthened the German defences.

The summer of 1942 saw the Germans fail to take or even isolate the strategic objective of Stalingrad. As winter approached, on 19 November Russian forces broke through having crossed the River Don and three days later broke through Romanian positions, completing the encirclement of General von Paulus' 6th Army. The commander of Army Group B, *Generalfeldmarschall* von Weichs, suggested that the troops fight their way out of the encirclement, making a strategic withdrawal. Once again, Hitler refused to consider the idea and demanded that the Luftwaffe conduct another air supply operation.

By this time, the situation was far worse than the previous year, with 300,000 troops having to be sustained. Such a large force needed a daily minimum of 1,500 tons of food and ammunition, with more needed if they were to make a fighting retreat. A force of 500 aircraft was needed, with little more than 250 Ju 52/3ms available. There were some more modern and larger aircraft, as well as gliders including the new Gotha Go 242, but in German service gliders made one-way trips. To make up the numbers, bombers were transferred to the airlift but in an example of appalling stupidity, the Germans assumed that the warload of a bomber would be the same as the payload when used as a transport. This ignored the lower density of supplies such as food and clothing and the difficulty of loading supplies into a bomber.

The weather also played a part and as the winter progressed, flying was not always possible. Even when it was, it was often necessary to warm the engines before attempting to start them by lighting fires underneath them. Usually, less than 30 per cent of the aircraft were available.

Instead of the 1,500 tons daily that was needed, the best daily delivery on 19 December was 289 tons, and over the period from 22 November 1942 to 16 January 1943, the average daily delivery was less than 100 tons.

Russian forces gradually tightened their hold on the beleaguered Germans but little attempt was made to free-drop or parachute supplies to the besieged troops, possibly because of growing Russian aerial superiority and intense anti-aircraft fire. On 2 February 1943 the inevitable happened, with 94,000 German and Italian troops surrendering to the Russians, leaving more than twice that number dead.

Generalmajor Fritz Moritz, who eventually became the Luftwaffe's air transport chief, was appalled by the waste of resources and stated firmly that before launching an airlift, 'every possible effort must first have been made to obviate the necessity for one.' It mattered little. From 1943 onwards the German air transport capability withered away.

Fortunately, the Allies maintained and even updated their air transport capability. A number of Allied prisoners in Germany were flown home but it was even more important in the Far East, given the distances involved. As Japan surrendered and the repatriation of Allied prisoners-of-war began, many were able to opt for air travel home rather than spend weeks on a troopship. The fact that so many ex-PoWs were opting for air travel home surprised *The Times*, which ran a story headlined 'Air Travel Preferred'.

The lessons were not lost on the military. With large garrisons of troops in the occupied territories of Germany and Japan, and for the United Kingdom many garrisons and bases across the Empire, air travel started to take over from troopships as the 1950s progressed. Gradually the troopships were withdrawn and one of them, *Nevasa*, found a new career as an educational cruise ship with paying passengers and schoolteachers in the former officers' accommodation and children in what had been the troop accommodation. 'Trooping by Air' was the new policy, both for servicemen and their families. Sometimes military transports were used but more often chartered civil aircraft were provided by airlines. In the UK this was a boost to the independent airlines that had already proved their worth in the Berlin Airlift (see below) but had an uncomfortable existence alongside the two big nationalized airlines, British Overseas Airways Corporation (BOAC) and British European Airways (BEA).

There were peacetime opportunities for transport aircraft to prove their worth. In Europe, the winter of 1946–7 was one of the harshest on record. The RAF's No. 38 Group was pressed into service, flying food and animal feed to remote villages isolated by heavy snowfalls. There was no AA fire to contend with but a Handley Page Halifax bomber engaged in this vital civil relief crashed in Staffordshire, killing all those on board.

On gaining independence from the United Kingdom in 1947, India was partitioned into two countries, India and Pakistan. While India itself was a complete single territory, albeit with offshore islands, Pakistan was divided into two from the outset with East Pakistan separated from the larger and more populous West by almost 1,000 miles of Indian territory. The Royal Air Force had used transport aircraft to move 30,000 refugees from communal strife in Pakistan to India upon independence; then post-independence the Royal Pakistan Air Force had to create an air-bridge between the two portions of the country. Initially this used Bristol Freighters which were later replaced but eventually the problem was solved when East Pakistan seceded and became the independent state of Bangladesh in 1971.

Into a Cold War
It soon became clear that the end of fighting in the Second World War did not mean that the world had returned to peace. Even as the war drew to a close, it was clear to many that the Soviet Union was taking the opportunity to extend its empire across Eastern Europe, while in the Far East, Japanese surrender had left two countries – Korea and Vietnam – divided, with what was to become a Communist north in each case. Before long, the enemies of yesterday – Germany, Japan and Italy – were the allies of tomorrow and the 'ally' of yesterday, the Soviet Union, was the new potential enemy. The Chinese Nationalists, backed by the West during the Second World War, were no longer threatened by the Japanese but by the growing power and success of their Communist rivals, so that eventually the Nationalists were driven offshore to the island of what is now Taiwan but for many years was known as Nationalist China.

The two sides in what became known as the Cold War created new alliances, with the North Atlantic Treaty Organization (NATO) formed by the Western democracies and the Warsaw Pact created by the Soviet Union from its East European satellite states. The West also created the Baghdad Pact, which became the Central Treaty Organization after a military coup in Iraq, and the South East Asia Treaty Organization (SEATO), formed by the UK and the USA with Australia, New Zealand and a number of militarily weaker countries in the Pacific Rim. Of all these alliances, only NATO has survived to this day.

The carve-up of Europe and South-East Asia by the rival power groups created many problems but nowhere more so than in Germany as the country was divided among the Soviet Union, United States, United Kingdom and France. The former's territory became East Germany, a Communist republic, while the other three territories came together to form West Germany, a democratic republic. If this were not complicated enough – since after all it simply mirrored what happened in Korea and Vietnam – the former German capital of Berlin, which was far to the east of the country, was also divided. East Berlin, the Soviet zone, became the capital of East Germany, while the Anglo-American-French zone became West Berlin, a city state.

Road and rail access to West Berlin ran through East German territory and was carefully monitored by the Russians and East Germans. The Soviet Union maintained that as Berlin was in East Germany, the entire city should be unified and governed by East Germany. The need to reform the currency used in West Berlin was the last straw. The East German government had no intention of allowing democracy in its area and having an outpost of democracy in West Berlin was yet another problem, for although not part of West Germany, West Berlin was emotionally tied to the West.

In retrospect, it seems little short of a miracle that the only direct clash between the armed forces of the superpowers was in Korea but, of course, the possession of nuclear weapons and later thermonuclear weapons by both sides in effect created an armed stand-off that endured for more than four decades. The policy may have been known as MAD ('mutual assured destruction') but there was a certain sanity and coolness of mind coming from it.

The Transport Aircraft Changes Shape

The political changes were accompanied by technical changes. Transport aircraft before the Second World War had mainly been fairly small, with the exception of some longer-distance flying boats. Passengers or goods boarded and disembarked through doors at the side. Some of the gliders changed this. A few broke open for easy unloading while others, such as the British Hamilcar, had nose doors so that vehicles could be driven off, prompting an American officer to describe it as the 'biggest chunk of airplane' he had ever seen. The German Me 321 was even bigger but with the same facility and this followed through into its powered variant, the

Me 323. Post-war, the British Bristol 170 Freighter bore a close resemblance to the Hamilcar.

Even more practical was the concept of rear doors, introduced late in the war by aircraft such as the Fairchild C-82, an aircraft with a twin-boom fuselage so that the tailplane was mounted at the end of two booms. This allowed for a rear door, which not only made loading and unloading vehicles easier, but it could also be opened in flight so that troops and equipment could exit quickly. A larger development, the C-119, first flew in 1947 and became widely known as the 'Flying Boxcar', although to the manufacturer it was known as the 'Packet'. Power could be boosted in this twin-piston-engined design by the addition of turbojets to help in taking off from high-altitude airfields or in very hot weather, when aircraft performance may be substantially diminished.

The French Nord Noratlas had a similar configuration but was smaller, while the British Armstrong-Whitworth Argosy had four turboprop engines but came along much later. The British Blackburn Beverley had a long tail stretching from the upper part of the fuselage in which up to seventy troops could be carried, leaving the rest of the aircraft available for up to 22 tons of freight. Slow and lumbering, this four-piston-engine aircraft did have a very good landing and take-off performance, claimed as being able to use a football pitch. The Douglas C-124 Globemaster could carry the same load but at a much higher speed and was easier to maintain, having a low wing.

Other changes were taking place as well. Not only did the United States Army Air Force become the autonomous United States Air Force in 1947 but the following year the new Military Air Transport Service was formed. This was part of the USAF but took over the aircraft and personnel of the Naval Air Transport Service.

The Berlin Airlift
The presence of a strong air transport fleet was never needed more than in the Berlin Airlift, possibly the greatest transport challenge of the Cold War and even beyond. It overwhelmed the air forces involved and required extensive chartering of commercial aircraft.

On 1 April 1948, the Soviet Union cut the railway link between West Berlin and West Germany, initially just for a couple of days. Then on 11 June, there was another one-day cut for the railway line but on this occasion road access was cut as well for two days, the excuse being that repairs had to be made to the Elbe Bridge. After what may be described as nuisance closures, on 24 June all freight and passenger transport to the city by road, railway or inland waterway was closed by the Soviet Union. The following day, a ban was imposed on all movement of food from the farms of East Germany to West Berlin. The purpose of the blockade was to force the Western powers to allow the Soviet zone to start supplying provisions and fuel to the entire city, thereby giving them practical control over it.

There were three air corridors linking West Berlin with West Germany, roughly linking the city with south, central and north Germany. Each corridor was 20 miles (32km) wide but there was an altitude restriction of 10,000 feet (3,048m), largely to prevent the corridors being used for aerial reconnaissance of the territory on either side and also to allow Soviet aircraft to overfly the corridors.

Even before the complete severance of all surface transport links, as early as 1 April the United States Air Forces in Europe (USAFE) had operated thirty flights by C-47s of the 53rd Troop Carrier Squadron from Rhein-Main, just outside Frankfurt, 275 miles (443km) to West Berlin along the southernmost of the three air corridors linking West Berlin and West Germany. The supplies were intended for the US army's garrison in West Berlin and the operation was intended to show that the United States was not prepared to submit to Soviet blackmail. However, the Russians were also prepared to show that they were in earnest and the C-47s were harassed by Yakovlev Yak-3 fighters during their flights.

Unfortunately, on 5 April a BEA Vickers Viking airliner flying along another corridor to Gatow Airport in West Berlin's British sector with ten passengers aboard was harassed by a Yak-3 fighter, which collided with the airliner at 1,000 feet (305m), leaving no survivors.

Being cut off from the West and from food supplies from East Germany, by 26 June West Berlin, with its population of 2.5 million people, had supplies of grain and flour sufficient for 17 days, cereal for 32 days, fats for 48 days, meat and fish for 25 days, potatoes for 42 days, and skimmed and dried milk for 26 days. There were some farms within the city limits, mainly with dairy cattle, but their output was not sufficient for the city's daily needs. To maintain the stocks of food, West Berlin needed 13,500 tons of food daily, including 646 tons of wheat and flour and 3 tons of yeast.

Clearly the only option was an airlift but the USAFE estimated that its own daily airlift capacity was just 700 tons and that even if strict rationing was imposed, a basic but adequate diet would still require 5,000 tons of food daily for the city. The same estimate indicated that the use of aircraft from other Allied air forces and chartering commercial transport could increase the daily airlift to 3,000 tons and the difference between this and the 5,000-ton daily requirement could be closed to some extent by boning meat and dehydrating potatoes, reducing the weight of these items by about 25 per cent.

The ensuing operation was known to the RAF as Operation PLAINFARE (with any puns no doubt intended), while the USAFE named it Operation VITTLES. These were not to be the only differences, as after the operation ended the USAFE calculated that the combined airlift had supplied the city with 2,323,067 tons, while the normally more conservative RAF calculated that 2,325,809 tons had been supplied. Only 30 per cent of the cargo flown into West Berlin consisted of food, with 60 per cent of it comprising coal. So that the economic life of the city could continue, the remainder was made up of raw materials for manufacturers, whose finished products were then ferried out from the city. One estimate was that for every 260 tons of raw materials flown in, 100 tons of manufactures were flown out.

The airlift was under way just two days after the final closure of the surface links but it was not an auspicious start. Limited by their 3-ton maximum load, the USAFE's C-47s managed to carry just 80 tons of milk, flour and medical supplies into Templehof, in the American sector, in thirty-two flights. On the previous day, the RAF had sent its first aircraft, eight C-47s, to Germany from their base at Waterbeach near Cambridge. The USAFE had a total of just 102 C-47s available, while the RAF believed that it could provide another 150 aircraft of all types. The French *Armée de l'Air* could only provide personnel, as its transport aircraft were already committed to the war in French Indo-China.

By 29 June, the USAFE had Nos. 60 and 61 Transport Groups carrying 384 tons of supplies to the city, while the RAF had fully committed Nos. 24 and 30 Squadrons, also with C-47s.

On the ground there was chaos. Some of the restrictions imposed by air traffic controllers were completely unrealistic, with those at Frankfurt insisting on a twenty-five-minute separation between flights to West Berlin. At Wiesbaden aircraft were parked nose to tail, while at Berlin they could wait up to an hour at Templehof before unloading. Just two return trips could take an aircraft and its crew up to thirty hours.

Fortunately, the British and American governments were determined that the airlift would succeed. On 30 June, Wiesbaden received the first of thirty-five Douglas C-54 Skymasters, gathered from bases as far away as Hawaii. Two squadrons of Short Sunderland maritime-reconnaissance flying boats from the RAF's 201 and 230 Squadrons, ten aircraft in all, were transferred from Northern Ireland to Hamburg, arriving at the old Blohm & Voss factory on 5 July ready for flights to West Berlin's Havel See. By 20 July, the RAF had these 10 Sunderlands, 40 Avro Yorks and 50 C-47s on the airlift, while the USAFE had 54 C-54s, later increased to 72, and 105 C-47s, with the 9-ton payloads of the Yorks and C-54s enabling the daily tonnage to pass 2,000 tons and then rise to 2,250 tons, with approximately two-thirds being carried by the USAFE and a third by the RAF.

Anticipating a long siege, construction of a new runway was started at Templehof, while at RAF Gatow, a runway that had been under construction opened on 27 July. In West Germany, or perhaps the 'mainland' end of the airlift, the RAF transferred its C-47s from Wünsdorf to Fassburg to reduce congestion.

Air safety was much worse at that time than today, not least because of the use of piston engines and gasoline rather than turbojets, turboprops or turbofans and kerosene. Given the frantic tempo of operations, some accidents were only to be expected, given the safety standards of the day. The first came on 9 July at Wiesbaden when a USAFE C-54 crashed, killing the two pilots and a USAFE civilian employee. On 25 July, a USAFE C-47 struck a block of flats in West Berlin; the two pilots were killed, although no record remains of any civilian fatalities.

That there were not more accidents was little short of a miracle as the Soviet Union was determined to do everything short of invading West Berlin, which would have risked all-out war. Anti-aircraft guns were fired 'on exercises' close to the three air corridors in a show of force and as a distraction to the air-crews. Then the Russians threatened to fly combat aircraft in the air corridors.

Harassment by Russian and East German forces was a feature of the airlift, with at least 700 cases recorded. In more than a hundred of these cases, searchlights were used to dazzle pilots at night and there were almost as many cases of aircraft flying too close, as opposed to 'buzzing' airlift aircraft, which occurred around eighty times. There were more than fifty cases of flares being fired at aircraft and balloons were used to obstruct flights eleven times. Ground fire struck airlift aircraft on fifty-five occasions. All of West Berlin's airfields were close to East German territory and the East Germans erected a transmitter mast on the approach to Tegel in the French sector of West Berlin. As all Allied troops had access to all of Berlin, the French simply sent their troops to blow up the mast.

What made the Berlin Airlift so unusual and spectacular lay in the variety of goods that had to be moved, many of which were ill-suited to air transport. Even today, air freight is best used for high-value goods, many of which are, by coincidence, lighter and less bulky. Bulk goods are best moved by railway, by sea or even by road and also tend to be relatively low-value. Moving coal and oil into West Berlin was as important as moving food but both these items were bulky and heavy and required specialized handling equipment which the airports at each end of the airlift lacked. Unloading sacks of coal or drums of oil or petrol was labour-intensive but the specialized freight-handling equipment one finds at airports today did not exist at that time. Indeed, the design and size of the aircraft of the day would have been ill-suited for such equipment in any case.

In an attempt to solve some of the handling issues, the USAF modified a Boeing B-29 Superfortress with coal loaded into the bomb bay, which opened as the aircraft made a low pass, dropping the coal. Unloading was quick enough but the experiment was a complete failure as the coal was reduced to dust on impact. There was no escaping handling coal the hard way: the first shipment was on 7 July with the coal loaded into barrack bags aboard the C-54s but despite this, on 8 July 75 per cent power cuts were imposed. This brought about some hardship with West Berlin's underground railway and trams cancelled after 18:00 each evening.

Oil transport required special aircraft as well as special unloading facilities, both of which were provided by a British company, Flight Refuelling, which supplied four Avro Lancastrian tankers, converted Lancaster heavy bombers, each of which could lift 1,500 gallons at a time. These were provided at a charter rate of £98 per flying hour and were the first of many civilian chartered aircraft. The rate offered was £45 per hour for a DC-3 or its military cousin the C-47, although the aircraft were smaller than the Lancastrian, which was a generous £8 an hour above the then prevailing rate on the air charter market. The higher rate was necessary, not just because of the high demand and the need to obtain sufficient aircraft, but also to cover higher insurance premiums, the higher cost of maintaining aircraft away from their home bases and accommodating personnel for an indefinite period. While most of the aircraft were ex-Second World War types, there were also some interesting and very useful new arrivals including the Bristol 170, more usually known as the Bristol Freighter, later becoming well-known for operating as cross-Channel car ferries. By contrast, there was also the sleek Avro Tudor of British South American Airways. In all some twenty-five airlines, some with only a single aircraft, joined the airlift.

Only British, American and French aircraft were allowed to fly in to West Berlin but the pressure on the RAF was eased by pilots being seconded from the Royal Australian Air Force, Royal New Zealand Air Force and the South African Air Force, with the RAAF pilots moving more than 7,000 tons of freight and more than 7,700 passengers.

All three of West Berlin's airports were used: Templehof in the American zone, Gatow in the British and Tegel in the French. Tegel was the least convenient of the three for the city centre. Despite the number of flights, stacking over West Berlin was avoided as far as possible due to the limited airspace available over the city and the need to avoid straying into East Berlin's airspace but also because military pilots and air traffic controllers were unused to this procedure. The USAF recalled reservists to its air traffic control units as they were likely to have the much-needed civil experience. Only RAF and USAFE airfields were used in West Germany as those of the *Armée de l'Air* were too far west to be of real use.

Pressure also manifested itself in other ways. Congestion at airlift airbases in Germany was such that Burtonwood in Lancashire was used for heavy overhauls, while the USAF set up a pilot training centre at Great Falls in Montana to prepare air-crew for the airlift and also recalled 10,000 reservists for air-crew duty. The USAF tried to minimize the use of the C-47 in favour of C-54s and an additional sixty of these larger aircraft were assigned to the airlift. The United States navy sent twenty-four R-5Ds, its designation for the C-54, while the RAF introduced its new four-engine Handley Page Hastings transports to the airlift.

There were further accidents as the airlift continued. Before the air traffic control systems were enhanced, two USAFE C-47s collided in thick fog near Ravolzhausen. On 19 September, a British Avro York crashed on take-off at Wünsdorf, killing all five crew members. An Avro Lancastrian tanker on a positioning flight for the airlift crashed on take-off at Thruxton in England with the loss of all seven on board.

On 5 August, the first manufactured goods were sent by air out of the beleaguered city. By 7 August, the daily airlift into West Berlin passed the 4,000-ton mark.

A demonstration of what could be expected from transport aircraft in the future came on 17 August when a solitary Douglas C-154 Globemaster flew 20 tons of supplies into the city on the first of twenty-four flights by this aircraft up to 24 September. Before it left, three Fairchild C-82s, predecessors of the C-119 Packets, joined the airlift; each was able to carry up to 5.5 tons but, more important, was capable of carrying bulky items such as steam-rollers and ambulances. On 18 September, to mark the

USAF's first anniversary (or 'Air Force Day') almost 7,000 tons were air-lifted into West Berlin in a special effort. Daily tonnages were still rising; however, flights were hindered but never completely stopped by the fogs of November.

That winter, desperate for fuel, West Berliners helped to fell trees in the forests surrounding the city but even so, a number of them died in the cold. Soviet pressure further intensified in April 1949 when West Berlin's cows were stolen, creating an additional problem, especially for those with young children.

The needs of young children were not ignored in the meantime. On 20 December 1948, just before Christmas, the USAFE mounted Operation SANTA CLAUS at Fassburg Air Force Base, carrying gifts for 10,000 children in West Berlin. The USAFE also mounted Operation LITTLE VITTLES, dropping sweets and chocolate to children, many of whom spent much time watching aircraft landing and taking-off from West Berlin's three airports. Some pilots tried to extend this to children in East Berlin but this was stopped after a few days by the USAFE.

On 11 April 1949 a daily record of 8,246 tons of cargo was airlifted, only to be surpassed on 16 April when a special effort code-named 'Easter Parade' lifted 12,490 tons.

On 12 May 1949, the blockade was lifted almost as abruptly as it had been imposed. Despite this, the airlift continued into the summer to restock supplies and as an insurance against the sudden reimposition of the blockade. The last flights took place on 16 August 1949.

The manpower needed for the airlift totalled around 75,000, of which 45,000 were German cargo-handlers. At its peak, there were 441 USAF aircraft, 147 RAF aircraft and 104 commercial aircraft. These provided a total of 277,804 flights, of which 189,963 were by the USAF, 65,857 by the RAF, many with Commonwealth crews, and 21,984 by chartered aircraft.

The Far East
Post-war, the colonial powers hastened to reclaim those territories that had been occupied by the Japanese in their rapid advance across the Pacific in 1941–2. The British were best placed for this, having returned to the Pacific with the largest and best-balanced fleet the country had ever sent to sea. For the Dutch and the French it was much more difficult, although the latter had never completely left their colonies in French Indo-China.

In the Netherlands East Indies, the territory was too large and too sprawling for the Dutch to have any real chance of returning to the pre-war situation. The Netherlands lacked the finance, equipment and man-power to undertake re-colonization and so Indonesia obtained independence in 1949 after a brief struggle.

In Indo-China, the French soon found themselves facing an opponent, the Viet Minh, that had strong support from the Communist Chinese. War was waged from 1946 until eventually the French surrendered in 1954.

The war in French Indo-China was marked by a growing use of air transport, both on assaults and penetration of enemy-held territory, and also for reinforcements and re-supply. As the Americans were to discover later, movement by ground transport during the war was hampered not just by a poor infrastructure, many waterways and dense jungle but also by the activities of the local guerrillas. Initially, the French used French-built Junkers Ju 52/3m transports, known to the *Armée de l'Air* as the AAC-1. These had been obsolete at the start of the Second World War and were too small and too slow compared to the Douglas C-47. It was not until 1952 that the AAC-1s were replaced by C-47s and the new Fairchild C-119 Packet, with around 100 of these aircraft in total stationed in Indo-China.

As in Burma during the Second World War, the French established bases behind enemy lines but in this case it was to mount counter-insurgency operations. One of the most ambitious of these was the taking of the valley of Dien Bien Phu, Operation CASTOR. This commenced with the flying-in of Airborne Battle Group 1 consisting of three parachute regiments and supporting units on 20 November 1953, using a large force of C-47s and C-119s. Later that day, Airborne Battle Group 2 was flown in with three more parachute regiments, again successfully despite difficult terrain surrounded by high ground. Two airfields were taken and one of these was devoted to the airlift of additional troops and supplies, and for the evacuation of the wounded. Despite reinforcements being flown in later, the Viet Minh forces in the area proved to be far stronger than expected and gradually began to close in, making landings at the two air-fields dangerous as aircraft came under mortar attack. Increasingly strong Viet Minh anti-aircraft fire also began to disrupt the re-supply missions and by early 1954, a third of all air-dropped supplies ended up in Viet Minh hands.

The outcome was inevitable, with the beleaguered garrison surrendering on 7 and 8 May 1954, bringing the war in French Indo-China to an end and leading to the creation of two states: Communist North Vietnam and pro-Western South Vietnam.

Meanwhile, another war had started in the Far East; this time between Communist North Korea and pro-Western South Korea. Korea had been occupied by Japan since before the First World War and with Japanese surrender was divided into two states. These were supposed to hold elections and combine into a single state but this never happened. The Korean War was one of the few supported by the United Nations, because the Soviet Union was boycotting the Security Council. In effect, the war was between the world's democracies and the Soviet Bloc.

On 25 June 1950, South Korea was invaded by troops from North Korea, with the invasion supported by air attacks. The first aircraft to be destroyed in the war was a MATS C-54, caught on the ground by four Yak-9 fighters as they attacked Kimpo Airfield.

The C-54 proved to be the mainstay of the American operation to airlift men and supplies from Japan into Korea, with the Pacific Division of MATS receiving an extra forty aircraft from its Atlantic Division and from the United States. Additional aircraft were provided from Australia, Belgium, Canada and the United Kingdom, with the latter providing the new Handley Page Hastings four-engined transport. As with the Berlin Airlift, the French were too heavily engaged with the war in French Indo-China to help. However, the RAF managed to join the Korean operation despite being stretched by counter-insurgency operations in Kenya and Malaya.

In Korea and Malaya, also later in Cyprus, extensive use was made of helicopters to move troops, especially over difficult terrain.

Peace in Indo-China lasted barely ten years before a new conflict broke out, with guerrillas from North Vietnam filtered into South Vietnam. Initially the United States provided so-called 'military advisors' for South Vietnamese forces but their numbers increased and gradually the United States found itself involved in the war; not only on the ground but also in the air and at sea, with US warships attacked by North Vietnamese forces.

In theatre, Fairchild C-123 Providers and Lockheed C-130 Hercules transports provided airlift within Vietnam, while other aircraft including the Lockheed C-141 Starlifter and C-5A/B Galaxy provided heavy lift. An air-bridge was established from the continental United States and Hawaii as well as Japan and Hong Kong into Vietnam. McDonnell Douglas C-9A Nightingales, derivatives of the DC-9 airliner, were used to evacuate the wounded back to the USA.

More than any other conflict, the Vietnam War became the war of the helicopter, especially the Bell 205, designated the UH-1 (utility helicopter 1) but known as the 'Huey' after its original designation of HU-1.

Humanitarian Relief

Air transport soon replaced the troopship in terms of moving personnel and their families, although its use declined with the granting of independence to many of the British colonies. Later, the end of the Cold War saw a reduction in the size of garrisons in what had been West Germany, as East and West Germany were united into a single state.

Air transport also became vital for humanitarian duties, flying emergency supplies and aid into areas devastated by hurricanes, earthquakes or tidal waves, or simply to areas affected by severe famine.

One of the first significant humanitarian missions took place in 1973, in Operation KHANA CASCADE which saw four RAF C-130 Hercules transports and a single Westland Wessex helicopter (the licence-built version of the Sikorsky S-58) engaged in famine relief in Nepal. Rice and grain were dropped to villages in West Nepal. This operation required the aircraft to fly low over razor-sharp ridges and then drop to just 200 feet (61m) above the floors of the mountain valleys, often in difficult weather, before discharging their valuable cargo. It was planned that the RAF would deliver 1,850 tons of cargo but 1,957 tons was delivered between 4 and 30 March, taking just half the time the planners had expected.

While an RAF spokesman described the operation in Nepal as the service's 'biggest since the Berlin Airlift', a much bigger operation was in store. In Ethiopia, the cumulative effects of drought and civil war led to a massive famine in 1984. Under pressure from the aid agencies, Western governments had to provide not just relief aid in the form of food and medical supplies but transport aircraft as well. The start of the operation was hampered by the Ethiopian government at first refusing to allow Western aircraft into its skies but after a change of mind, the Ethiopians demanded even more aircraft. Even then, an Ethiopian government minister demanded that the RAF should land and unload supplies rather than drop them in the areas where they were needed and where runways, or even landing strips, seldom existed.

It took from summer until early winter to resolve these issues, so Operation BUSHEL did not commence until 1 November 1984. Seven RAF Hercules were needed, with two actually flying relief missions from a forward base at Addis Ababa while another five acted as reliefs and flew spares from the UK. The operation had been due to last for three months but was extended to late 1985, by which time the Luftwaffe had based C-160 Transalls at Addis Ababa and even Warsaw Pact countries had decided to participate using Antonov An-12 transports and Mil Mi-8 helicopters. The International Red Cross also chartered a commercial Hercules in September 1985. The two RAF aircraft accounted for 30 per cent of the relief aid delivered.

The civil war meant that one difficulty hindering operations was that aircraft could not be based at Assab, the port through which most sea-borne supplies entered the country, but had to make a positioning flight from Addis Ababa to Assab each morning before starting the day's relief flights.

During the three decades that have passed since the relief flights over Ethiopia, air transport capability has grown further, despite defence cuts following the end of the Cold War. Many air forces now have transports such as the Boeing C-17 Globemaster III with a 45-ton payload, while in both commercial and military use are aircraft such as the Antonov An-124 with a 150-ton payload, although this is always discharged on the ground and not from the air. Such large aircraft also mean that it is easier to transport helicopters to wherever they are needed, quickly and relatively easily.

Chapter 18

Heavy Lift

Before the Second World War, aircraft were seen as frail machines and only capable of moving relatively light loads. However, their potential for freight was clear from the early days and during the 1920s, British troops in Mesopotamia, modern-day Iraq, were not only moved around by air but also supplied by air.

Armies require much heavy equipment. Lightly-armed troops are vulnerable, which is one reason why the use of paratroops has declined since the Second World War. Most wartime aircraft loaded through a side door and handling even light artillery pieces or small vehicles such as Jeeps was difficult and time-consuming. That also meant that the aircraft and those working around them were vulnerable to attack while they were on the ground.

It did not help the development of transport aircraft that so many air forces still clung to the concept of an aircraft that could double up as a bomber and a transport, even in the 1930s when the more forward-thinking designers had already started to see these as two completely different requirements. The RAF had the Bristol Bombay, which first flew in 1935, while the Luftwaffe had the famous Junker Ju 52/3m trimotor. There was also the compromise position of bombers and transports using the same aerodynamic surfaces, i.e. wings and tailplane. The Vickers Viking used the same design of wings and tailplane as the Wellington bomber, while the Avro York used the same design of wings and tailplane as the Lancaster heavy bomber.

In pre-war Germany, the restrictions imposed by the Treaty of Versailles on aircraft manufacture, especially military aircraft manufacture, saw many bombers developed as transports, including the Dornier Do 17 known to the RAF as the 'Flying Pencil' and which must have been a very uncomfortable and cramped airliner!

The Glider Shows the Way
Oddly enough, it was the unpowered glider that led the way towards transports that could carry heavier and bulkier loads and not simply carry them, but also see them unloaded quickly. This was despite the fact that

gliders were viewed by many as being light and simple aircraft that required little in the way of strategic materials to build, had less time-consuming and demanding training for pilots, and of course had to be towed off the ground by powered aircraft.

The pioneering work on military gliders for uses other than elementary training took place in the Soviet Union during the mid-1930s. Earlier in Germany, gliding clubs had been used as a means of re-establishing a military air arm and circumventing the restrictions imposed on the country by the Treaty of Versailles. It was Germany that first used gliders to transport troops, using the DFS 300 which was designated an 'attack glider'. The DFS 300 was first used in this role on 10 May 1940 in the capture of the vital Belgian fortress of Eben-Emael and three bridges over the River Meuse. Later, gliders were used to take the bridge over the Corinth Canal in Greece during the Balkan campaign and then for the invasion of Crete, where heavy losses were suffered by glider-landed forces and paratroops. Crete was the last of the major glider operations as Hitler was reluctant to authorize any further airborne operations because of the heavy losses. However, gliders were still used for smaller operations including the re-supply of German forces beleaguered on the Eastern Front.

As mentioned in the previous chapter, gliders were also used to re-supply Allied forces fighting in Burma, where for the first time gliders were able to make a return journey by being 'snatched' off the ground by low-flying transport aircraft acting as tugs.

However, gliders were never a completely reliable answer to the problem of moving large numbers of troops and considerable amounts of equipment cheaply as there were many risks involved. These were most apparent during Operation HUSKY, the Allied landings on Sicily, when 137 gliders were used but in poor weather 60 of them landed in the sea.

Nevertheless, the British Airspeed Horsa glider showed a marked step forward, capable of carrying twenty-eight fully-equipped troops or a howitzer or light vehicle such as a Jeep. Unloading was made much easier and simpler by a variant of the Horsa that had cordite charges capable of blowing off the glider's tail. This was known as the 'surcingle'. Others had wires and cutters that could achieve the same end. There were also versions with hinged noses that swung open so that vehicles could be driven out but this was not as popular as might be expected as glider noses were especially prone to damage on landing.

Plans to build a powered version of this all-wooden aircraft were never fulfilled. It was an improvement on the earlier British General Aircraft

Hotspur which was cramped, although to increase capacity there was the 'Double Hotspur' with two fuselages bound together by a section of aerofoil.

Another glider that could also carry Jeeps was the American Waco CG-4A, known to the RAF and the other Commonwealth air forces as the Hadrian. Almost 14,000 CG-4As were built, of which just over 700 were supplied to the UK. It could carry up to thirteen fully-equipped troops or items such as a howitzer or a Jeep. The CG-4A accounted for a significant share of the total of 16,000 gliders built in the United States during the war. The most impressive American glider was the CG-17, which was a C-47 with a fixed undercarriage and without engines but with the engine nacelles intact and faired over. This had the largest capacity of any American glider and, if necessary, could have engines fitted so that it could become a C-47 if this proved necessary!

Two gliders – one British, the other German – pointed the way towards the future for moving heavy items by air.

The largest production wooden aeroplane of the war, the General Aviation Hamilcar, was described by American officer Colonel Frederick Dent, in charge of the USAAF glider procurement programme, as 'the biggest chunk of airplane I have ever seen put together.'

Behind this large aircraft was the British realization that if air-landed troops were to be used in any large-scale operation, they would need more than just light arms and they would also have to be landed in considerable numbers. The Hamilcar was first flown in half-scale form in 1941 but the full-sized glider could carry up to sixty fully-equipped troops or cargo up to 18,000lbs, which meant that two armoured cars or a light tank could be landed. Despite its bulk, it could be towed by a Short Stirling or any other heavy bomber and its 150 mph (240 kmph) towing speed was on a par with any other glider. Clamshell doors in the nose made loading and unloading easy. As with many gliders, the undercarriage was jettisoned after take-off and landing was on skids, although later versions retained the undercarriage to make ground-handling easier after landing. A very practical touch, given wartime conditions, was that the engines of any vehicles aboard could be started before landing, with the fumes exhausted through a pipe running to the glider's exterior, so that within fifteen seconds of landing, armoured cars or tanks could be rolling off the glider. Vickers designed the lightweight Tetrarch tank especially for glider-borne operations. A twin-engine powered version was also built, the Hamilcar X, but this does not seem to have been deployed operationally.

The largest glider ever built was the Messerschmitt Me 321 *Gigant*, which was also probably the ugliest ever built. Like the Hamilcar, it had large clamshell nose doors that opened to facilitate the loading and unloading of bulky items. Designed for the invasion of England, the *Gigant* could swallow either a heavy tank, a tractor, an 88mm anti-tank gun, or carry up to 200 fully-equipped troops on two decks. First flown on 25 February 1941, even though empty, the Junkers Ju 90 tug had great difficulty in getting the *Gigant* airborne and it was usually towed off by three aircraft. Later, two Heinkel He III bombers known as the He IIIZ were combined with an intervening aerofoil in which there was a fifth engine for use as a tug. Sometimes rockets were used to help get this massive glider into the air.

Rather more practical, more than 200 Me 321s were converted into powered transports; these had six engines and were designated the Me 323. They were just in time for the evacuation of the *Afrika Korps* from North Africa and on one flight more than 240 troops were airlifted out.

A rival to the Me 321 was the Junkers Ju 322, planned as an all-wood glider but needing 8 tons of steel to ensure rigidity. The flight test programme showed little promise and the final problem that ensured abandonment of the project occurred when a light tank was loaded and then fell through the Ju 322's wooden floor!

Post-War Developments

The wartime experience showed that aircraft could be used for carrying heavier loads and that this would be a useful feature, not just in military operations but for commercial applications as well.

One of the first aircraft to meet this need was the Bristol 170 Freighter, some of which appeared in time for the commercial airline contribution to the Berlin Airlift. While what was then the Royal Pakistan Air Force used a number of these for its air-bridge between East and West Pakistan, the aircraft is best remembered for its vehicle ferry services across the English Channel and for livestock operations between New Zealand's North and South Islands.

More significant and widely-used was the Douglas C-124 Globemaster, capable of carrying up to 25 tons over long distances. This made a brief appearance on the Berlin Airlift – given its capacity, no doubt many felt that it was all too brief – but the aircraft was still to enter widespread service at the time. While the Fairchild C-119 Packet (or 'Flying Boxcar') and the Nord Noratlas twin-boom aircraft also contributed to airlift capability, they lacked the 'big load' capacity of the Globemaster, as indeed did the Bristol Freighter. Anxious to increase capacity and range on their car air ferry services, one airline converted a number of DC-4s with the flight deck repositioned above the fuselage, as with the Boeing 747, so that clamshell doors could be fitted. Known as the 'Carvair' and capable of flying cars and passengers from southern England as far as Switzerland, these nevertheless proved not to be a commercial success.

Another aircraft with limited use was the Blackburn Beverley, a heavy-lift aircraft capable of lifting 22 tons and with a good short-field performance but which was slow and only ever used by the RAF.

The demand for heavy lift nevertheless continued unabated and a number of aircraft were specially designed for this role. The need was not simply military, with companies engaged in construction and energy exploration and production, especially in remote areas with poor ground communications, also providing a good market. Other needs have been the movement of power-plant turbines and railway locomotives: one of the latter movements with securing chains and a section of track comprised the world's heaviest air cargo consignment to date at over 150 tons.

Nowadays the big heavy-lifters are the American Lockheed Martin C-5B Galaxy and its rival, the Ukrainian Antonov An-124 *Ruslan*, each with a load capacity of around 150 tons. The An-124 is in commercial use but, like the C-5B, was designed to meet a military need, in this case the transport of ballistic missiles for the former Soviet Union of which the Ukraine was a part. Only the USAF MATS operates the C-5B but the smaller Boeing C-17 Galaxy III is in use with many air forces including the RAF and the RAAF as well as there being a NATO pool of these aircraft with their 45-ton payload.

The need for heavy lift, or at least the movement of difficult loads to remote locations, has seen other ideas come to the fore. One of these has been the use of airships (or dirigibles) but these become increasingly difficult to handle as size increases and the need for lighter-than-air qualities also means that they must grow in size and volume as the payload is increased. Some hope has been placed in using airships that are only slightly lighter than air once loaded but need forward movement to lift off; however, many of the problems with a standard airship still remain.

Ever-larger helicopters have also been in demand and this need saw developments such as the Sikorsky S-64, or in US service the CH-53 Flying Crane, while in the Soviet Union Mil produced ever-heavier helicopters such as the Mil Mi-6 'Hook' and the even larger twin-rotor Mil Mi-26 'Halo', capable of lifting up to 20 tons. Nevertheless, while lifting capability by helicopters is useful, with Kaman in the USA providing a small helicopter for this role so that loads can be transferred, true heavy-lift capability for helicopters comes at a high price and also comes with a relatively low speed, short range and high fuel consumption.

This leaves the two largest helicopters in widespread use as the Boeing CH-47 Chinook twin-rotor heavy-lift helicopter, a development of the earlier CH-46 Sea Knight or Ranger, and the rival single-rotor Sikorsky S-65, also designated as the CH-54 Sea Stallion. The original CH-54 had twin engines but an upgraded variant known as the Super Sea Stallion has three engines.

Chapter 19

Ejection Seats

Escape from an aircraft about to crash became progressively more difficult as speeds rose and this was at first primarily a problem for fighter pilots. The Royal Air Force advised pilots flying the Supermarine Spitfire to push back the cockpit canopy, invert the aircraft, undo their seat belt and 'eject' from the aircraft. The Fleet Air Arm for some reason found this difficult with the Seafire (the naval variant of the Spitfire) and instead pilots stepped out onto the wing but this could be tricky, especially if the pilot was wounded, and there was always the danger of a pilot being badly injured or even killed if he hit the tailplane of his own fast-moving aircraft. This was not a peculiarity of British aircraft as one German fighter ace, *Oberleutnant* Hans-Joachim Marseille, lost his life in this way.

Oddly enough, one company that invented and developed the first ejection seats was an airframe manufacturer whose products never entered production, although the Martin-Baker MB-5 was claimed by its manufacturer to be the fastest piston-engined fighter of the Second World War, capable of 460mph (736kmph). Sir James Martin had started his own aircraft company in 1929 with the financial support of Captain Valentine Baker from 1934. In 1934 he was commissioned by the Air Ministry, the parent government department of the Royal Air Force, to design an ejection seat as it was clear that aircraft speeds were already too high for a conventional escape in mid-air. The problem was clearly going to worsen with the advent of jet fighters.

However, the first jet fighter pilots had to cope without an ejection seat, for it was not until 24 July 1946 that the first manned ejection was made from a Gloster Meteor jet, an achievement for which Martin was knighted.

From the beginning, ejection seats involved the use of two explosive charges underneath the seat, with the first breaking the connection with the aircraft and the second propelling the seat and pilot out of the aircraft, after which the pilot would leave the ejection seat and deploy his parachute to drift safely to the ground or the sea. More modern ejection seats are often rocket-propelled and able to correct any imbalance from the attitude of the aircraft at the time of ejection. The pilot is now cast out of the seat automatically and parachute deployment is also automatic. Since the first ejection seats were introduced, variants have been produced that work at zero altitude, allowing for problems during take-off or landing and that work underwater. Some ejection seats have canopy-breakers on the back; others rely on the aircraft canopy either being thrown open or being burst in a controlled explosion.

The provision of ejection seats is not just limited to the pilot of an aircraft as the observer or navigator on a modern two-seat fast jet also has one. However, the large heavy bombers of the 1950s and 1960s could only provide ejection seats for the two pilots as provision for other crew members would have weakened the structure of the aircraft. The pilots were meant to keep the aircraft in the air while the other crew members scrambled out through a hatch, which was usually in such a position that there was no risk of being struck by the tailplane. Even turboprop intermediate trainers now have ejection seats for both student and instructor.

An alternative to the ejection seat has been to have the cockpit in a module that could separate from the aircraft and parachute to earth, as in the General Dynamics F-111.

Practical problems have prevented the application of ejection seats to helicopters as these would require a device to shear off the rotors. Considerations of weight and cost have prevented ejection seats being applied to light aircraft, although a few types do have built-in parachutes to enable them to reach the ground safely if they have an engine failure; however, many would be able to glide to the ground more safely.

Clearly the ejection seat has no place in an airliner, as apart from the weight and cost, it would be impossible to design an airframe strong enough to cope with the numerous hatches that would be needed for the system to work. That is also apart from possible premature use by nervous passengers! Additionally, there is the point that aircraft ejection seats are far from comfortable.

Chapter 20

Search & Rescue

While the potential of the aeroplane for search and rescue was recognized early on, what was originally known as air-sea rescue effectively dates from the Second World War. Before this, there was always the chance of a flying boat of what was originally RAF Coastal Area (later RAF Coastal Command) being diverted for search duties. However, there was little in the way of a dedicated search-and-rescue organization other than that of the largely volunteer Royal National Lifeboat Institution (RNLI), which has the world's most densely located network of lifeboat stations around the entire British Isles.

During the Second World War, air-sea rescue was divided between RAF Fighter Command and RAF Coastal Command. The split meant that search and rescue (SAR) in coastal waters was the responsibility of Fighter Command, while in the open seas it was the responsibility of Coastal Command. A number of aircraft became synonymous with SAR, including the Supermarine Walrus and Sea Otter and the Grumman Goose. The RAF also operated a Marine Branch with rescue launches to augment the work of the RNLI and continued to operate these with officers recruited from the Merchant Navy until 1985.

In the United States, such duties belonged to the United States Coast Guard (USCG) service, although this was part of the United States navy in wartime. The USCG used, and continues to use, a mixture of aircraft and cutters for SAR.

The Luftwaffe used the Focke-Wulf Fw 58 *Weihe* ('Harrier'), a twin-engine advanced trainer, for search and rescue, supported by fast launches. The *Weihe* was capable of dropping life-rafts to downed airmen and there was also a floatplane variant, the Fw 58W, which could pluck downed airmen from the water.

The appearance of the helicopter with its ability to hover soon showed that this was the ideal machine for search and rescue. The early helicopters such as the R-4 were of limited use, only being able to accommodate two men, but the Sikorsky S-51 Dragonfly (or R-5) was capable of winching people up from the sea or from the deck of a ship. Eventually, as larger helicopters appeared, permanent SAR flights were positioned at major military air bases. While their original *raison d'être* was the rescue of military airmen, increasingly their workload became primarily civilian and not always at sea, as rescue in mountainous areas or in the aftermath of flooding also became an important part of their work.

The need for long-range SAR meant that during the Second World War, and for some time afterwards, converted bombers were used and at one time it was usual for these to carry lifeboats that could be dropped for survivors to board. In more recent years, inflatable life-rafts that inflate on contact with water have become a much more practical provision.

Picking up survivors may require considerable skill as in many cases they are too weak to help themselves, either through injury or through hypothermia as a result of overlong immersion in water. One early solution was the use of a net at the end of the winch line but today it is more usual for a winch man to descend to pick up the survivor while a colleague handles the winch controls. The Royal Navy used qualified divers in this role for many years so that if anyone was trapped inside an overturned boat, they could dive under it and rescue them. However, this useful provision has now been lost as a result of defence cuts.

In the United States, search and rescue was mainly the province of the USCG but the USAF's Military Air Transport Service also provided SAR helicopters including the Sikorsky S-65 or, in military guise, CH-54, the largest SAR helicopter in service today. In the UK, SAR was divided between the Royal Air Force and the Royal Navy with the former being the major provider. However, as military air stations closed, work was increasingly transferred to the Coastguard, using helicopters chartered from commercial operators. In the near future, all service SAR helicopters will be replaced by Coastguard helicopters operated by a commercial contractor. The UK's SAR facilities have been seriously compromised by the withdrawal of its long-range maritime-reconnaissance aircraft. In the USA, not only are the US navy's long-range maritime-reconnaissance aircraft used to augment search and rescue but many USCG air stations have Lockheed C-130 Hercules with surface-scanning radar to support longer-range search and rescue.

Another type of rescue that has developed has been combat rescue, which came into being during the Vietnam War and is still mainly a USAF service. This involves escorting the rescue helicopters, often with armed attack helicopters such as the Apache and even having armed troops on board, to rescue downed pilots in territory that is either contested or occupied by the enemy.

SECTION THREE

ON THE GROUND

Overview

The early years of the Second World War with German armies smashing their way west and then east were the days of the tank, especially the German *Panzer* or armoured divisions. Yet the tank was not a product of the Second World War but instead had been born in the First World War. However, the Second World War tank was a far more formidable beast than that of just over twenty years earlier and came in many more versions, such as light tanks that could be air-landed by gliders and specialized tanks for mine-clearing or destroying major fortifications, but the fact remains that it was a creation of the First World War and the impasse that lasted so long on the Western Front. In a similar way, the machine gun and the concept of trench warfare were not creations of the First World War but, like the use of barbed wire and railways for transporting troops, stemmed from the American Civil War. There were also other inventions such as flame-throwers but these are not much in evidence today and so cannot be counted as a 'legacy'.

Valuable forces such as the Special Air Service can trace their history back to the Second World War but the use of lightly-armed and highly-trained and motivated troops is something that can be dated back to the Boer War and possibly beyond, as the SAS could be said to have turned guerrilla warfare on its head.

What did emerge from the Second World War on land was refinement. Troops were much better equipped to do whatever was expected of them and better trained to use that equipment. For example, the Normandy landings could not have happened in the First World War, so it was fortunate that the British Expeditionary Force was not driven back into the sea. Although the evacuation at Dunkirk could have been managed during the First World War and with much less loss of life, the return to France could not have been managed. One only has to look at the great difficulties faced in the landings at Gallipoli to see how much changed during the Second World War.

It became possible for armies to cope with difficult terrain and severe weather due to all-wheel-drive vehicles, while landings were made easier by amphibious vehicles, as were river crossings. Coordination between air and ground forces was improved immeasurably during the war and this is a legacy that continues to this day with no army of any consequence lacking its own air power.

The real problem in looking at the Second World War's military legacy on the ground is that some of it really belongs to the air forces and some to the navies. This was a splendid blurring of the lines. On the other hand, one cannot say that forces became air-minded during the Second World War because many of the air arms operating in the First World War were part of their country's army and those that were not were part of their country's navy; at least until 1 April 1918 when the autonomous Royal Air Force was created from the Royal Flying Corps and the Royal Naval Air Service. Many other countries followed suit but not the United States, which did not establish its own autonomous air service until 1947, although that did not stop the United States Army Air Force behaving as if it was autonomous, having many of the same ideas about its roles as the RAF! By contrast, the autonomous Luftwaffe, much favoured by Hitler as well as by his air minister Göring, behaved as if it was an arm of the army and lacked strategic vision, as did the Red Air Forces of the Soviet Union.

Chapter 21

Four-Wheel Drive

Four-wheel drive was known before the Second World War but it was the war that brought it into widespread use, most notably with the famous American Willys Jeep.

The first recorded patent for four-wheel drive was by the British engineer Bramah Joseph Diplock in 1893; however, this was not for a motor vehicle but instead was intended for steam traction engines. Later, Diplock produced a track-laying vehicle, more usually known today as a caterpillar vehicle. His work was inspired not by the need to cover rough terrain or cope with conditions such as snow or heavy mud but an attempt to design a vehicle that would not damage the public highway, a persistent problem with steam-powered road vehicles. His four-wheel-drive vehicle had four-wheel steering, three differentials and his 'pedrail' wheel, designed to cope with difficult road surfaces.

Before the turn of the century, in 1899 Ferdinand Porsche designed and completed a four-wheel-drive electric vehicle in Vienna and this was exhibited at the 1900 World Exhibition in Paris. The Porsche four-wheel drive was designed for a wagon manufacturer, the Hofwagenfabrik Ludwig Lohner & Co., and obtained four-wheel drive by having an electric motor at each wheel, making the vehicle very heavy. It did nevertheless show good acceleration for the day. It became known as the Lohner-Porsche but the use of four motors meant that it was not recognized as being the first four-wheel-drive motor vehicle.

True to what would now be regarded as a four-wheel-drive motor vehicle was the Spyker 60 HP, which was also the world's first six-cylinder-engined car. It was built in 1903 by two brothers, Jacobus and Hendrik-Jan Spijker, who lived in Amsterdam; this was a two-seater sports car and intended to be a hill-climber. It still survives to this day and can be seen at the Louwman Collection at The Hague.

By this time, work on four-wheel drive was also in progress in the United States and Germany. An American company, Twyford, built six such vehicles in 1905 and 1906, one of which still exists. In 1908, the Four Wheel Drive Auto Company, confusingly known as FWD (the term normally used for front-wheel drive), produced a prototype lorry and later some 15,000 of its Model B were built for the British and American armies during the First World War. A rival was the Nash Quad, which also had four-wheel steering.

Meanwhile, the German Daimler-Motoren-Gesellschaft, more usually known as Daimler-Benz, produced its *Dernburg-Wagen* in 1907 and this also had four-wheel steering. This was used by a German colonial official working in what is now Namibia but was then a German colony. Between the two world wars, Mercedes-Benz and BMW produced a series of four-wheel-drive and four-wheel-steering vehicles. However, the constraints of finance and materials meant that during the Second World War the most common German light passenger vehicle was the Volkswagen Beetle-based *Kübelwagen*, meaning 'bucket car', which was an apt description of this open vehicle. The *Kübelwagen* had two-wheel drive from its rear-mounted air-cooled engine.

The age of the four-wheel-drive vehicle really began with the Jeep, designed to meet a demand from the United States army for a general-purpose 'go-anywhere' vehicle. It is believed that the pronunciation of the military designation of GP (for Government Purposes or General Purpose) led to the popular name of Jeep, which Willys, the main manufacturer, registered in 1950. During the Second World War, Willys and Ford produced 653,568 Jeeps, which the US army's chief of staff, General of the Army George Marshall, maintained was the country's greatest contribution to modern warfare. The Supreme Commander, Allied Powers in Europe, General Dwight D. Eisenhower, thought that it was one of three tools that together won the war for the Allies, the other two being the C-47 transport aircraft and the landing craft.

The Jeep had permanent four-wheel drive, basic seating for four and was usually left-hand drive. It was rugged and fulfilled the promise of a 'go-anywhere' vehicle but had poor stability, especially when turning. The original Jeeps were always petrol-engined as the day of the small diesel suitable for cars was yet to come.

With the return of peace, Willys decided to continue building the Jeep and in 1945 started to market the CJ-2A which was available for general sale, including to private owners.

Short of materials for its traditional up-market cars due to post-war allocation of materials by the British Ministry of Supply, British motor manufacturer Rover decided to attempt a vehicle that was an improvement on the Jeep, offering better stability and better accommodation for passengers and goods. The result was the Land-Rover, with permanent four-wheel drive and differential lock for use when wheels started slipping, aluminium bodywork and three-abreast seating. The three-abreast seating caused Land-Rover to consider placing the steering wheel in the middle to avoid having to build both left- and right-hand-drive versions but this was rejected as impractical.

Launched at the 1948 Amsterdam Motor Show, despite chronic under-investment in production facilities, the new product soon outsold Rover's cars and gained a worldwide reputation. A wide variety of bodies was produced and the Land-Rover was available in both short and long wheelbase versions.

Willys' successor, Kaiser Jeep, produced a developed version of the Jeep in 1963. Known as the Wagoneer, it introduced independent front suspension and automatic transmission to four-wheel-drive vehicles but more obvious to the onlooker was that for the first time a four-wheel-drive vehicle was finished as a passenger car. Later, luxury four-wheel-drive vehicles were produced and these were known as sport utility vehicles or SUV. Production passed first to Rambler in 1970 and then to Chrysler when that company acquired Rambler's parent, American Motors Corporation (AMC).

Meanwhile, Land-Rover introduced its own more luxurious four-wheel-drive vehicle, the Range Rover, using a Rover 3.5-litre V8 engine based on an American design. While the original Land-Rover had been aimed at the military and at farmers, the Range Rover was aimed at the more affluent, as well as the police who could use it as a utility or pursuit vehicle. While the original Range Rover had an interior that could be hosed down, before long more luxurious interiors became standard and engine capacities were increased, as well as having diesel options and automatic gearboxes. As the Range Rover moved even further up-market, vehicles that fitted in-between the Land-Rover and Range Rover were introduced, starting with the Discovery and then the smaller Freelander, followed by a smaller Range Rover, the Evoque.

One Land-Rover that received adverse publicity in the UK was the Snatch variant. This was essentially a long-wheelbase Land-Rover with a van-like body, lightly armoured to provide the occupants with some pro-tection from small-arms fire and roadside explosive devices. Originally intended for patrols in Northern Ireland, many were deployed to Iraq and Afghanistan where the armour protection proved inadequate, especially when confronted by so-called improvised explosive devices (IEDs), essen-tially home-made and often remotely-detonated roadside bombs.

Technology had moved on. There was more to an effective military 4 × 4 vehicle than simple off-road capability and four-wheel drive. Experience, originally against terrorists in South Africa, had shown that the shape of a vehicle's undersides had a profound influence on the way it reacted to mines and roadside bombs. A V-shaped base on a vehicle deflected much of the force of an explosion around the sides rather than into the vehicle.

This has led to a new family of vehicles for patrol and carrying personnel. Smallest of these is a direct successor to the Snatch Land-Rover known to the manufacturer, Force Protection Europe (US-owned but based in the UK), as the Ocelot and to the British army as the Foxhound; a small, substantially-armoured, four-wheel-drive vehicle. Next up in size is the US Ridgeback, built by Force Protection in the USA, a development of the United States army's Cougar and a substantial four-wheel-drive vehicle weighing almost 19 tons. Its larger cousin is the Mastiff, a six-wheel-drive vehicle, also closely related to the Cougar and weighing around 28 tons. These variants all have V-shaped armoured undersides. One reason for having a family of three vehicles is that the Ridgeback can be used in confined spaces such as urban streets in which the Mastiff would be too unwieldy and cumbersome.

Other manufacturers were building SUVs by this time and today every major manufacturer has at least one SUV model in its product range. Improvements were made to enhance reliability and also ensure that power was directed to the wheel or wheels that made best use of it. Many of the newcomers did not provide full-time four-wheel drive but retained this as an option, leading to them being known as 'crossovers', to reduce wear and tear on tyres and other components as well as reducing fuel consumption.

There were also a number of manufacturers who introduced four-wheel drive using other systems such as Jensen with the Ferguson Formula (or FF) version of its Interceptor touring saloon. Such models were not intended for off-road work or for utility but simply to improve road-holding at speed and were derived from racing cars.

For military and commercial use, four-wheel-drive lorries were also produced, notably including the Unimog produced by Mercedes-Benz.

However, not every need could be satisfied simply by having four-wheel drive and the need for larger vehicles saw the introduction of six-wheel drive. One of the first such vehicles was the amphibious DUKW, pronounced 'duck', produced for the United States army and Marine Corps by Sparkman & Stephens and the General Motors Corporation

(GMC). The official name DUKW was an acronym: 'D' denoted the fact that it was designed in 1942; 'U' stood for utility; 'K' for all-wheel drive; and 'W' denoted dual rear axles. There is more on the DUKW in the next chapter, which deals with amphibious vehicles. The DUKW's capacity was around 2 tons and it could carry troops as well as equipment. It was larger than the Jeep and its amphibious capability was naturally another advantage.

Also amphibious was the Alvis Stalwart, introduced to the British army in the early 1960s and which also had six-wheel drive. Like the Land-Rover, it came from a manufacturer better-known for its cars, and indeed Alvis was a high-quality, low-volume manufacturer of cars with hand-built bodywork. It was part of a family that included other six-wheel-drive vehicles such as the Saladin, Salamander and Saracen armoured cars and personnel carriers but these did not share its amphibious qualities. The load that could be carried was a useful 5 tons or 10 tons could be towed, and the Stalwart had twin-steer, meaning that the two front axles were steerable. The cross-country capability was impressive, largely because all six wheels were driven at the same speed and there was only a limited differential to allow the inner and outer wheels to move at different speeds during cornering. The problem was that this made for difficulties when driving on a normal surface, with the simple bevel gear system causing what is known in multi-wheel-drive circles as 'wind up', meaning that there was stress between the components. So the Stalwart was highly capable off-road but needed considerable maintenance. Whenever the amphibious capability was not needed, it was removed to ease maintenance and reduce the vehicle's weight. Today, the British army has four-wheel-drive lorries that are much simpler and easier to maintain.

The Soviet Union and its client states have also used eight-wheel drive for armoured personnel carriers rather than tracked vehicles as used in the West. The largest of these is the BTR-60 (P). Amphibious, it also differs from the British and American equivalents as the occupants can fire through ports in the side, whereas British and American infantry dismount from the AFVs (armoured fighting vehicles) in order to fight. Six-wheel-drive AFVs supplied by the Soviet Union include the BTR-152, the tyre pressures of which can be varied by the driver while on the move.

For many people today, four-wheel-drive vehicles have become a status symbol. Known by the press and by the authorities as SUVs, they are commonly known in the UK as 'Chelsea Tractors', reflecting the fact that many are never driven off-road but that drivers like the high driving position and all-round visibility. Most armies still have four-wheel-drive vehicles with good ground clearance, not only as Land-Rovers or the equivalent but also as lorries and artillery limbers. These are far less complicated than the Alvis Stalwart and much better suited to intensive use as a result. The US armed forces also use the Humvee or 'Hummer' (derived from the acronym HMMWV for High Mobility Multipurpose Wheeled Vehicle), which is wider than the Land-Rover and as a result sometimes restricted in its usefulness.

Chapter 22

Amphibious Vehicles

Amphibious vehicles, or more simply amphibians (although the latter term clashes with aviation nomenclature for an aircraft that can touch down and take off on water or land), enable their operators to cope successfully with terrain in which land and water are interwoven and without bridges. It follows that many of them have a good off-road capability. However, amphibious warfare may be conducted without amphibious vehicles as landing craft or landing ships are not amphibious but simply enable troops, artillery and vehicles to come ashore safely on a beach. Hovercraft, provided they depend on heavy rubber skirts rather than sidewalls, are amphibious but are a post-war invention. A motor vehicle with very high ground clearance that can ford shallow waters is not regarded as being amphibious.

While there were experiments with amphibious carriages, the first practical applications date from the steam age and from the 1870s logging companies in the USA and Canada were using steam-tugs known as 'Alligator' tugs that could move over dry ground to get from a river to a lake or vice versa. This was an important factor as it avoided the cost of assembling tugs in the forests and the great difficulty of moving them across land in undeveloped areas with little or no infrastructure.

Interest in amphibious vehicles continued between the two world wars, often resulting in vehicles that were boats with wheels or attempting to waterproof the chassis of a motor vehicle.

It was not until the Second World War that more practical applications were developed and put into production, mainly in the United States and Canada. The first of these – resurrecting an old name – was the Alligator, officially designated as 'land vehicle, tracked' (LVT), and was an amphibious tractor developed from vehicles used for rescues in the Florida swamps. These were used in the Pacific theatre to carry personnel across mud, swamps or coral reefs, while others – armoured and armed – gave covering fire.

Next came the DUKW (pronounced 'duck'), and as already mentioned this was produced for the United States army and Marine Corps by Sparkman & Stephens and the GMC. First used in the landings in Sicily,

Operation HUSKY, DUKWs were also used in the attack on the Scheldt Estuary and in the crossing of the River Rhine. More than 20,000 were built, of which around 2,000 were passed to the British under Lend-Lease. The Canadians also produced a form of tracked amphibious vehicle known as the Buffalo, and again this was used in the Scheldt campaign.

Amphibious tanks were also created, known generally as 'DD' tanks (duplex drive), and usually based on the American Sherman tank although Valentines were used for training; these could be launched offshore to provide support for the first wave of infantry. They used large canvas flotation collars that looked like a canvas and metal fence and displaced enough water to provide buoyancy. In addition to their tracks, such tanks had propellers at the rear and were also useful for river and canal crossings.

One problem with the amphibious tanks was that they needed more space aboard the 'landing ships, tank' (LSTs) than conventional tanks because of the large flotation collar. Typically, an LST that could carry nine Sherman tanks could only carry five amphibious tanks. There were also limitations on their amphibious capability as the tanks had only been tested in waves a foot high (0.3m), but on D-Day on some of the beaches the waves were 6 feet (1.8m) high. Most tanks had enough air to allow the crew to survive for five minutes under water and thus have time to escape but there were also life-rafts carried on board.

A British attempt to create an amphibious truck, the Terrapin, was unsuccessful. The Germans produced an amphibious version of the previously-mentioned Volkswagen *Kübelwagen* but this was used only for reconnaissance against Soviet forces after the commencement of Operation BARBAROSSA, the invasion of the Soviet Union, being used on Russian lakes and rivers. The Germans also built an amphibious tractor but few of these entered service.

While the DUKW was cheaply-built and only intended for a short spell of combat duties, many survived the war. Some of those that were 'demobbed' into civilian use were used as water-buses at tourist venues, or in one case by fishermen to transfer their catch from the trawler to the fish market, thus reducing the time taken to get the catch to market. Others were used by emergency services for flood relief purposes. These vehicles certainly lasted far longer than the designers and builders had planned.

The post-war world saw plans for much-enlarged DUKWs, including the large BARC ('barge, amphibious, resupply, cargo'), but few were built. The Soviet Union built a copy of the DUKW with the refinement of a rear-loading ramp and 2,000 of these were supplied to the country's armed forces, remaining in service until 1962.

Many post-war tanks and armoured personnel carriers had a limited amphibious capability, mainly to help them cross rivers and lakes, with their tracks providing propulsion although some also had water-jets. The extent to which these could be used depended on the steepness of the banks on either side of the crossing. Nevertheless, amphibious vehicles were now suffering competition from the growing capabilities and availability of the helicopter.

Part of the problem was that the need for amphibious capability depended on the terrain, while increasingly four-wheel-drive vehicles were fitted with items such as a snorkel that enabled them to continue fording water, even if it covered the engine air intakes.

Amphibian interest revived during the Vietnam War, with the United States using the amphibious and articulated Gama Goat and the larger M520 Goer trucks, ideal for the many rivers and creeks and, of course, paddy-fields. However, these had a very limited speed of around 20 mph (32 kmph) on land. The US also had the HEMTT (Heavy Expanded Mobility Tactical Truck), the LARC-V (Lighter, Amphibious Resupply, Cargo, 5-ton) capable of moving 5 tons of cargo, and the much larger LARC-LX, with the latter able to handle 60 tons. Meanwhile, the Russians built a succession of amphibious vehicles including the GAZ 46 and BAV 485.

In the United Kingdom, in the early 1960s the British army received the first of its Alvis Stalwarts, the six-wheel-drive lorries described above. These used water-jet propulsion to give a speed of up to 6 knots. As previously mentioned, their cross-country capability was impressive, largely because all six wheels were driven at the same speed and there was only a limited differential to allow the inner and outer wheels to move at different speeds during cornering. However, difficulties when driving on a normal surface meant that the Stalwart was highly capable off-road but required considerable maintenance.

A big step forward came with the invention of the hovercraft: a true amphibious vehicle, providing that sidewalls were not used to contain the cushion of air and flexible but more vulnerable and easily-damaged rubber skirts were used instead. The United States Marine Corps is steadily moving towards using only hovercraft as landing craft as these can travel faster than conventional landing craft and need not stop at the water's edge but continue some way inland, providing the terrain is not too steep or uneven.

Chapter 23

Ground-Air Coordination

Although from the earliest days armies had used balloons with the objective of providing support and guidance for ground troops and artillery, the arrival of the aeroplane made coordination more difficult. Ground commanders had to wait for a plane to land before discovering what it had seen; although occasionally messages could be dropped, this was not always reliable. Directing aircraft to a different target as conditions on the ground changed was another problem, especially as fighters and fighter-bombers were often single-seat aircraft and pilots had neither the time nor the skills to quickly send a Morse code message or to decipher one. There were other complications. When the British tried to stop the famous 'Channel Dash' by the battle-cruisers *Scharnhorst* and *Gneisenau* with the heavy cruiser *Prinz Eugen*, their response – slow, tardy and bedevilled by excessive secrecy – was further affected by the fact that some ground stations were using wireless telegraphy while the aircraft were using plain speech radio.

German forces, using the blitzkrieg strategy of fast-moving and integrated ground and air forces, managed to avoid confusion by giving air-crews strict instructions before starting a mission, with the ground forces following quickly upon the bombing. Ground commanders, especially those in the elite *Panzer* armoured units, knew better than to get too close to the bombing.

The first time the Allies really engaged in fast-moving warfare was in the Western Desert campaign from late 1941 to 1943. The British had, up to this time, been mainly concerned with air power as a strategic resource, with tactical air power given far lower priority. In many ways, as the war was to prove, this was something that stood the British and the Americans in good stead. The Germans had failed in the Battle of Britain and even more so in the blitz on British cities because the Luftwaffe was not equipped for strategic air warfare and for some time lacked heavy bombers, and when they did come they arrived in insufficient numbers.

Yet, as the Battle of France showed with the poor performance of the RAF's Advanced Air Striking Force (AASF) and the British Expeditionary Force's Air Component, the British had also missed a trick and defeat in

France was all the more certain for the RAF's inability to react quickly, bombing major military objectives before the Germans could install strong anti-aircraft defences. It was clear that tactical and strategic air power each had an important role to play in warfare.

The air war in North Africa did not start until Italy entered the Second World War in June 1940. While the Royal Air Force was giving priority to the air defence of the United Kingdom, it was inevitable that what was then known as RAF Middle East Command was kept short of aircraft and that those it did have were far from being the most modern. RAF Middle East Command became even more short of aircraft when many of those it did have were transferred to Greece where they suffered severe losses, losing even more of the few that managed to get to Crete with just seven aircraft returning to North Africa. Prior to this, the RAF had been on its way to attaining air superiority in North Africa with the Italian *Regia Aeronautica* being far less well-equipped than the Luftwaffe.

In October 1941, the RAF established the Western Desert Air Force (WDAF) under the command of Air Marshal Sir Arthur Coningham and from the start a new phase in air-ground cooperation began as the WDAF headquarters and that of the British Eighth Army were located together. It was clear that this was to be a fast-moving theatre of war with a front line that moved some 1,500 miles (2,414km) over inhospitable terrain.

The WDAF was an international formation with South Africans being the most numerous of its personnel and later it included USAAF squadrons. Getting such a mix of nationalities to work together as an efficient and effective air force was one thing, but it was something else for it to become known for its mobility, moving airbases, or more accurately airstrips, as needed, and its ability to work closely with army personnel. It was not unknown for an aircraft to take off on a sortie and then afterwards land at a fresh airstrip closer to the front line than the one from which it had taken off. It helped that as its numerical strength grew, it was also supplied with more modern aircraft.

The close liaison that arose from having the ground and air force headquarters together was extended down to squadron level and it was made clear that the overwhelming priority of the WDAF was the support of ground forces.

The WDAF later became part of the Mediterranean Allied Tactical Air Force for the Sicilian campaign and then accompanied the Allied armies as they advanced through Italy.

The lessons learned provided the template for the Allied Expeditionary Air Forces created ready for the Allied landings in France, with the US

1st Allied Tactical Air Force and the British 2nd Allied Tactical Air Force staying with the armies and eventually even having their final operational bases inside Germany. The Supreme Commander, Allied Powers in Europe, General of the Army Dwight D. Eisenhower, had as his second-in-command a Royal Air Force officer, Air Chief Marshal Sir Arthur Tedder.

Much had been learned.

Chapter 24

Jerry Cans

The use of small cans for carrying petrol or diesel was a necessity for any army with road vehicles but those used by the British army at the outset of the Second World War were shoddy and of limited capacity. Indeed, at one stage their design and construction rendered them suitable for use during only one trip and these became colloquially known as 'flimsies'.

During the North African campaign in 1941 the British Long Range Desert Group captured many German fuel cans, which were larger, more robust, better-designed and far more practical and durable. As these originated from the Germans, nicknamed 'Jerries', it seemed natural to call them 'Jerry cans' but as the preparations for D-Day started, a member of the Combined Operations headquarters staff managed to persuade the British to start manufacturing them.

The basic design still remains in use today, unaltered.

SECTION FOUR

AT SEA

Overview

It is tempting to think that there was nothing new at sea during the Second World War. The submarine had appeared before the start of the twentieth century. The all-big-gun battleship appeared in 1906 with the British HMS *Dreadnought*. The aircraft carrier appeared in 1918, again in the Royal Navy, first with HMS *Furious* and then HMS *Argus*. The first purpose-designed aircraft carrier, HMS *Hermes*, appeared in 1922.

Certainly, for some navies, little had changed between 1918 and 1939. The Japanese radar systems lagged behind those in Europe and North America, while the Imperial Japanese Navy (IJN) lacked sonar. The Italian navy had to avoid night battles, if it could, also lacking radar. Neither Germany nor Italy could get an aircraft carrier into service, although this also reflected inter-service rivalry and politics as much as the technical challenges involved.

Even the Royal Navy, that had developed the aircraft carrier and by 1939 had the finest aircraft carriers of the Second World War on order, lacked high-performance aircraft aboard its ships. Senior naval officers did not believe that high-performance aircraft could operate from carriers. The Royal Air Force, which between the wars was responsible for naval aviation until May 1939, had been doing its best with poor funding until the last couple of years before war broke out. RAF control of naval aviation was the basis of the problem. The pioneers of British naval aviation who were still serving in 1939 had been transferred to the Royal Air Force. Some of them reached air rank, the equivalent of the Royal Navy's flag rank or general rank in the British army, and there were too few senior officers who understood aviation or who had seen the level of aircraft development enjoyed by the United States navy. Yet, there was also much else to learn.

One of the big problems that had not been solved during the First World War was how to put an army ashore on an enemy-held coastline. The problem had in fact grown since the First World War because by 1939, the British army was mechanized and had tanks. The same had happened in the United States. The only major amphibious landings in the First

World War had been at Gallipoli and these had been a disaster, starting badly and getting worse.

Sonar was only developed at the end of the First World War, as anti-submarine warfare during that conflict had relied on hydrophones, the efficiency of which was compromised by the noise of the machinery and propellers (strictly speaking, these should be called screws) of the ship using the apparatus.

Minesweeping during the First World War was a hazardous business, requiring the minesweeper to pass through the minefield pulling a para-vane that would cut the wire connecting the mine to the seabed. The mine would then float to the surface and be destroyed by gunfire. Magnetic mines were not deployed until 1918 by the Royal Navy but no one knew how to sweep them. During the Second World War, magnetic mines and pressure mines were finally tackled.

Anti-aircraft operations from warships in the First World War consisted of using the ships' lighter weapons and while between the wars much had been done to develop improved high-angle (HA) guns, recognizing the growing threat from the air, the importance of anti-aircraft defences was still underestimated.

Chapter 25

Landing Ships and Landing Craft

There is nothing new about amphibious warfare. It was brought to an advanced stage of sophistication during the Second World War but many lessons had to be learned during the war years. The Japanese have generally been regarded as the earliest exponents but in Europe it dates from before the Battle of Marathon in 490 BC. Even the Norman invasion of England that culminated in the Battle of Hastings in 1066 showed little improvement over earlier years. Troops had to scramble over the sides of their ships as they ran aground and then run through the surf up to the beach. At Hastings, success was due in part to superior Norman tactics but also due to the fact that the defending army led by King Harold had been force-marched south from their victory over the Vikings at Stamford Bridge in Yorkshire and were almost certainly less able to fight well than their adversaries.

One of the biggest amphibious operations before the dawn of the twentieth century was the Walcheren expedition of August 1809, when the Royal Navy landed what was for the time the considerable force of 40,000 men on the island of Walcheren using 520 transports escorted by 42 ships of the line (predecessor of the battleship), 25 frigates and 60 smaller vessels under the overall command of Rear Admiral Strachan. The Dutch port of Vlissingen was captured but an assault on Antwerp failed and the troops suffered heavy losses before being re-embarked.

While the First World War is best remembered in Europe for the protracted offensives and bloody battles on the Western Front, another abiding memory of the war is in what has been variously known as Gallipoli for the land war and the Dardanelles for the war at sea. This was at the outset a major amphibious operation.

Few now realize that there was a plan for an even more audacious amphibious operation that would have meant nothing less than the sea-borne invasion of Germany herself, with landings on the Baltic coast of Pomerania, the closest point to the capital, just 80 miles from Berlin. Both this aborted plan and the Gallipoli landings had one thing in common: they were attempts to break the stalemate on the Western Front.

On the morning of 25 April 1915, the invasion of Gallipoli started with 1,500 men of the Australian 1st Division, disembarked from the battleships into small boats, which were towed by small steam pinnaces towards the beach. First light came at 04:05 and the pinnaces cast off their tows at 04:25, leaving the boats to be rowed towards the shore by sailors. It was at this moment that the first fire came from the defenders: initially badly-aimed, it became increasingly accurate as the light improved and the boats closed on the coast, but most of the first wave reached the beaches safely.

Elsewhere, an innovation was the use of an old merchant ship, the *River Clyde*, with doors cut in the sides of the hull so that a large number of troops could land quickly, running across a bridge of lighters. The lighters were towed into place by a tug but almost immediately began to break away in the strong currents, only being held together by the prompt action of a commander and an able seaman who dived into the water and held the lashings secure. As the first of 2,000 men of the Munster Fusiliers and the Hampshire Regiment ran through the doors, they were immediately cut down by a well-planned and well-aimed burst of Turkish fire. About half the men were caught on the pontoon bridge, the other half remaining inside the ship, and machine guns mounted in her bows were used to stop the Turks from advancing onto the beaches.

The Second World War

Initially, the amphibious landings of the Second World War showed little progress over earlier years. Despite coming under heavy fire and losing the ship carrying their headquarters organization at Oslo, the German invasion of Norway was largely a question of transporting troops into harbours. There was also an element of this at Copenhagen, although the main thrust into Denmark was over the border with Germany. The invasion of Norway was also supported by the arrival of air-landed troops.

At the 1941 Battle of Crete, the Germans used barges but the seaborne element of the invasion was savaged by the Royal Navy. However, it lost control of the air due to a shortage of fighters of any kind and the island was won by a costly German airborne invasion. So costly in terms of paratroopers, in fact, that for a while Hitler refused to sanction further airborne assaults.

Had Operation SEA LION, the planned German invasion of the United Kingdom, gone ahead, the Germans would have used barges and the Royal Air Force's Bomber Command devoted much effort to bombing these as they were assembled in French and Belgian Channel ports.

Something better was needed. While the British had recognized the need for special shallow-draught vessels for the abandoned landings on Germany's Baltic coast during the First World War, it was not until the 1920s that the United States Marine Corps started work on specially-designed landing craft. Further work was done in Japan, gaining pace during the 1930s. The thinking at the time was that troops would be carried in modified troopships capable of carrying landing craft and would then be transferred to the landing craft for the run ashore. The Japanese built the first specially-designed landing ship for the landings at Tientsin. This was the *Shinsu Maru* (*Maru* meaning 'ship'), developed from whaling factory ships. At the same time, they also started building the *Dai-Hatsu* type of landing craft, the first to be mass-produced with a landing ramp in the bows and which would be copied by both the British and the Americans in the Second World War.

The idea of a landing ramp in the bows was long overdue. This made disembarkation much quicker and easier, and in an assault on a defended beach, speed also helped to ensure success and reduce losses to enemy fire. In short, landing craft with bow ramps were safer but never completely safe. The first hazard that had to be overcome, ideally by beach reconnaissance, was that of grounding on a sandbar or a bar of shingle, when the ramp would be dropped and soldiers, burdened with heavy equipment, would run 'ashore' only to find that they stepped off the sandbar into deeper water and drowned. If that didn't happen and the beach had indeed been reached, as the troops left the landing craft it became lighter and drew less water, so could be swept by the tide and any wind over the troops that had just disembarked. These craft were in any case stern-heavy, not just to ease themselves onto the beaches but also because all the machinery and fuel was located aft.

Landing craft and landing ships became some of the most important types of shipping during the Second World War. No previous conflict had involved so many amphibious assaults. In the European theatre alone, there were major amphibious assaults by the Allies in North Africa where troops landed at three different locations because of part of the territory being in Spanish hands; also at Sicily, Salerno, Anzio and then, after the Normandy landings, the south of France. Later, there were the landings on the Dutch island of Walcheren and, of course, the crossing of the Rhine. This is ignoring such minor affairs as the taking of the islands of Lampedusa and Pantelleria. In the Pacific theatre, it is almost impossible to list the landings as the United States army and United States Marines island-hopped their way across the Pacific and eventually towards Japan.

Perhaps the greatest amphibious landing of all, had it occurred, would have been on the Japanese home islands but the use of the atomic bomb at Hiroshima and Nagasaki and the eventual Japanese surrender made this unnecessary. Just as well, as it would surely have been the bloodiest battle in history.

Nevertheless, this is to skip ahead by at least a couple of years. In 1940 when Winston Churchill became prime minister, he called for combined operations but only a handful of landing craft were available. There were two basic types: Landing Craft Assault (LCA), capable of carrying an infantry platoon, i.e. around thirty men, ashore; and Landing Craft Mechanized (LCM), that could carry just one tank or road vehicle. The Americans, not in the war at this stage, were even worse off, having just the Higgins boat which was a 36-foot wooden craft designed for civilian use by Higgins, a New Orleans boat-builder. These had powerful engines for their size and could be easily moved off a beach after grounding ashore but the early versions did not have ramp bows and the first use of such craft with this necessary modification was by the British and Canadians in the Dieppe raid.

Early raids used converted cargo ships, designated Landing Ship, Infantry (Large) (LSI (L)) and cross-Channel ferries designated LSI (M). These carried landing craft on derricks that were lowered into the sea. The start of specially-designed landing ships came with the Landing Ship, Stern-chute (LSS) and the Landing Ship, Gantry (LSG). The former had landing craft ejected down a stern chute, almost the reverse of the whaling factory ship that had the whale carcasses hauled up a stern chute. The British designed the ultimate in landing ships, the Landing Ship, Dock (LSD), which flooded a stern hold to allow landing craft or amphibious vehicles to float from its stern.

These designs were ideal for amphibious landings from the open sea and over long distances from the base for an assault. Inevitably the British had a much shorter-range attack in mind, the landings in northern France, which would need a landing craft capable of operating shore-to-shore. The distances were not long, varying between 22 miles and 80 miles (35km and 129km) depending on where the assault was to be made, and valuable time could be saved if landing craft did not have to be launched into the water. The British started preparing for this need with the Landing Craft, Tank (LCT) which varied in length between 112 and 225 feet, with no fewer than eight types being built. The LCT used at Normandy was the Mk 4, designed with the shallow shelving beaches of the Normandy coast in mind, and this carried six medium tanks. This design was mass-produced in the United States and became the Allies' standard vehicle-carrying landing craft.

For the Dakar expedition, three shallow-draught oil tankers were converted into Landing Ship, Tanks (LSTs) and each could carry eighteen Churchill tanks. These were also used for the invasion of Madagascar and again for the North African landings, Operation TORCH. The latter event showed that many more of these ships were needed so that armour, artillery, vehicles and troops could be put ashore quickly and in sufficient strength. Operation TORCH also showed that the Higgins boats were inadequate and these began to be replaced with steel Landing Craft, Vehicle, Personnel (LCVP). The design of the British LST conversions was adapted by the Americans for the 300-feet-long LST Mk 2, of which more than 1,000 were built and were in use in all of the major landings in Europe from Sicily onwards and in the Pacific they were first used at Bougainville, although they proved too slow to stay in a convoy. This led to the development of the 203-foot Landing Ship, Medium (LSM), first deployed in 1944.

Other American designs included the prefabricated 158-foot Landing Craft, Infantry (Large) (LCI (L)), which could carry up to 200 men for a forty-eight-hour voyage. Instead of a ramp, the bows had two gangways on either side. The LCI (L) was supplied to the United Kingdom and the Soviet Union under Lend-Lease. A British development, built of wood, proved vulnerable during Operation OVERLORD, the Normandy landings.

Landing craft were converted for a variety of roles, including rocket-firing ships, LSM (R), and Landing Craft, Flak (LCF), to provide additional anti-aircraft cover. The LSM (R) could carry 1,040 rockets and reload in forty-five minutes, giving it the fire-power of a light cruiser.

Post-war, landing craft remained essential to any country likely to engage in amphibious assault. The LSD remains in use with many navies, with most able to operate helicopters as well and the best designs can accommodate helicopters as well as landing craft. The British used their two LSDs during the Falklands campaign of 1982, although one of them had to be hastily refitted after spending time in reserve.

Chapter 26

Frigates

Few navies today manage without frigates, which have developed into the naval 'maid of all work'. The United States navy has allowed its frigate numbers to run down, largely because of ever-tighter defence budgets, and this is something that will only be partially alleviated by the new Littoral Combat Ship (LCS).

As with so much else, the history of the frigate pre-dates the Second World War by many years but this type of warship had disappeared long before the outbreak of the First World War and was reinvented to meet the needs of the Second.

The original frigate was a smaller warship than the ships of the line, too small to be positioned in the line and too lightly-armed. Nevertheless, these ships offered speed and manoeuvrability. By the eighteenth century, they were generally three-masted and although sometimes having the overall length of a ship of the line, had just one or occasionally two gun decks compared to the three of ships of the line. The Royal Navy stipulated that they had to have at least twenty-eight cannon. Principal duties included patrolling and convoy escort, and often a frigate would be despatched to a trouble-spot, perhaps to assist in putting down an insurrection.

Although definitely not a ship of the line – predecessors of the twentieth-century battleship – during a major sea battle frigates had an important role to play. Ships of the line were literally just that, with opposing fleets confronting each other in long lines. This meant that ships could only see the signals hoisted by the ship ahead and if a manoeuvre was hoisted, by the time the signal was relayed to the last ship, the line was broken. To ensure that signals were seen by all ships at the same time so that all could make the same manoeuvre at once, frigates were stationed abeam of the line to re-transmit any signals hoisted to all ships in the line that could see them at the same time. In this way, order was maintained.

In the middle of the nineteenth century, armoured and steam-powered warships began to appear and in the Royal Navy and the French navy, these ships evolved out of frigates as guns were carried on one continuous deck rather than being spread over two or three. Such ships soon became more powerful than ships of the line and it can be argued that these were the true predecessors of the battleship rather than the old wooden 'three-deckers'.

As the turn of the century approached, the supremacy of the big ships was threatened by the fast torpedo-boat: small, cheap to buy, economical in its use of manpower and, worst of all, something that many smaller navies could afford. This caused much the same consternation among the larger navies as did the fast missile-carrying boat in the latter half of the twentieth century. The solution was the torpedo-boat destroyer, also small and fast. This became the warship on which many future senior officers learned their command skills. Another new ship was the cruiser. To the Royal Navy any ship that patrolled or cruised was a cruiser but the term also began to apply to a reasonably well-armed ship, much smaller than a battleship and actually varying widely in size, with light cruisers being smaller than a destroyer of today but armoured cruisers were heavier. The light cruisers acted as a protective screen for battleships.

In short, by the late nineteenth century, the frigate had been squeezed out by a host of new arrivals.

Unlike the First World War when, for the first time in centuries the Royal Navy abandoned convoys and convoy protection until 1918, the Second World War saw convoys introduced immediately. In the First World War, the U-boat threat had not been fully understood and the Royal Navy thought that convoys would simply attract U-boats, failing to realize that this was the only means of getting them into an area where they could be found and attacked. However, convoys weren't a completely problem-free solution, since they not only needed strong protection but also meant that port facilities and storage were stretched upon their arrival. One week there might be nothing and the next everything would be packed, with yet more ships waiting to enter port for unloading or loading.

The successor to the frigate by this time was the destroyer which had, on average, more than doubled in size since the First World War and was armed with two or more turrets with guns of 4in or higher-calibre, plus torpedo tubes and depth-charge rails. They also had an anti-aircraft armament. Cruisers had also grown in size and these two types of warship had become the 'maids of all work' of the day.

Cruisers were sometimes deployed on convoy protection, especially the ex-First World War cruisers converted to act as anti-aircraft ships, but they were often used to track enemy surface-raiders or as a screen for battleships.

Destroyers were wasted on convoy protection. They could not use their high speed on convoys that often moved at less than 5 knots, although, of course, if a submarine was detected they had to move quickly in pursuit. Being lightly-built, destroyers sometimes suffered damage when in mid-ocean and their narrow beam also meant that their stability and sea-keeping was poor. It was not unknown for battleships or cruisers to send their destroyer screen back if the weather was bad enough.

There was a need for something slower and sturdier and the answer was the corvette. This design originated from the British Admiralty, which took the design of a whaler, ships built for the worst that the oceans, especially the Southern Ocean, could throw at them, stretched the design and adapted it to carry a light armament including anti-aircraft and anti-submarine weapons. The corvette proved to be just the right ship at the right time, or at least almost. The truth was that it was still too small and conditions aboard were arduous for a ship's company that could expect to spend several weeks crossing the Atlantic at convoy speed.

Larger than a corvette and more heavily-armed, the frigate came back, initially mainly as an anti-submarine warship but anti-aircraft frigates also appeared. These distinctions continued after the Second World War with the destroyer continuing to grow in size, some having eight guns in four turrets, and remaining as a general-purpose warship. A new category of frigate arrived in due course with the Royal Navy having the *Salisbury*-class aircraft direction frigates working in conjunction with the strike aircraft flying from aircraft carriers.

The continued development of the destroyer with anti-aircraft and anti-submarine missile systems and their increasing cost meant that something smaller and cheaper was required. The late 1950s saw the arrival of the general-purpose frigate with anti-submarine and anti-aircraft arma-ment, sometimes missile-based as with the Australian Ikara, sometimes using depth-charge throwers or mortars or anti-submarine torpedoes and usually with 4.5in main armament as well. There were still differences, with the British Tribal class capable of carrying a party of Royal Marines for colonial policing duties, operating alongside a true general-purpose frigate in the form of the *Leander* class. Both these classes carried small shipboard helicopters. In Canada the Royal Canadian Navy, which soon became the Maritime Command of the short-lived Canadian Armed Forces, went a stage further and some of its ships carried two Sikorsky S-61 Sea King anti-submarine helicopters. It was not until the arrival of the *Broadsword* class in the early 1980s that the Royal Navy obtained frigates capable of carrying two helicopters and these were the smaller naval version of the Westland Lynx, albeit the outstanding small-ship helicopter of its day. The Lynx could engage small fast-moving surface vessels as well as carrying anti-submarine torpedoes. The first batch of *Broadsword*-class frigates also had Exocet surface-to-surface missiles instead of a gun as their main armament but the lessons of the Falklands campaign of 1982 showed that a gun was more important as troops ashore needed the help of naval gunfire.

Today, most navies have a number of frigates that can fairly be described as general-purpose. The more recent have stealth character-istics, giving them the radar image of a much smaller vessel such as a fishing boat. Admiral Nelson is supposed to have complained of 'a want of frigates' and there is no doubt that many navies would like to have many more than they do today. Once again, whenever there is a need to display a naval presence for whatever reason, it is usually a frigate that is despatched at short notice.

Chapter 27

Improved Fleet Train

The fleet train is the term used for the ships that keep warships supplied and refuelled when at sea. Uniquely, the Royal Navy's fleet train is the Royal Fleet Auxiliary and is part of the Merchant Navy rather than of the Royal Navy itself. The reason for this is that the ships, registered as merchant vessels, can visit ports that might be closed to naval vessels or place restrictions on them as in wartime when the time a naval vessel can spend in port is limited to forty-eight hours.

The Royal Fleet Auxiliary consisted of just ninety-two ships, completely inadequate for the wartime size of the Royal Navy, and was almost completely committed to the Atlantic and Mediterranean theatres. When the Royal Navy returned to the Far East, it was at first heavily dependent on American ships, although this was minimized by the use of refuelling anchorages away from the battle zones with ships rotated out of line every few days, especially in the case of aircraft carriers with a heavy need for refuelling because of the continuous operations by their aircraft.

Working with the United States navy was a revelation for the Royal Navy in the Pacific. British tankers had refuelled warships by the in-line method, with the receiving ship under way astern of the tanker, using a system that took several hours and could only work successfully in good weather. The Americans used the abeam method, which was both faster and less dependent on good weather. Post-war, the Royal Fleet Auxiliary adopted the American system. Today, this has been enhanced by the use of helicopters carrying underslung loads to speed the transfer of dry stores between auxiliary and warship. One consequence has been that the RFAs, as the ships are called, now have mixed Royal Navy and Merchant Navy crews with the RN personnel manning the helicopters, the latter also being used for anti-submarine protection and surface-to-air guided missile systems.

Chapter 28

Sweeping Influence Mines

Using mines against enemy ships dates from the 1840s and during the Second World War mines were laid by both sides; both defensively to protect ports and harbours from enemy raids and offensively against the enemy's shipping. It is estimated that around half a million mines were laid during the Second World War but these were not as successful in sinking ships as expected, accounting for just 6.5 per cent of all shipping being sunk, much less than the success rate of aircraft, warships and submarines. However, the impact was much greater than this statistic implies as German mines closed British and even US ports for days and helped contribute to the siege of Malta. In 1941, a Finnish minefield in the Baltic hindered operations by the Soviet navy.

Mines could be laid by ships or by aircraft, with the Royal Air Force naming their mine-laying 'Gardening' and dropping mines on canals and rivers as well as ports and shipping lanes.

Most of the mines laid by both sides were the moored contact type: these were cylindrical balls fitted with horns, contact with which caused the mine to explode. These were generally swept by minesweepers towing paravanes, also known as Oropesa sweeps, which cut the wire keeping the mine moored and when it floated to the surface it was detonated by gunfire. Later, chains were used that could not be cut by the sweeps. Sweep obstructors were also used: small conical explosive devices that would destroy a sweep before it reached the mine.

Contact mines had been used from the beginning of mine warfare but at the end of the First World War the magnetic mine made its appearance. This was the first of what have become known as 'influence mines' and include magnetic mines, detonated by the magnetic field of a steel ship passing; pressure mines, which detonate as water pressure increases when a ship passes over them; and acoustic mines, which react to the sound of a ship's machinery or propellers. While contact mines were laid by ships – usually mine-layers but other types of warship could be fitted with mine-laying rails – influence mines could be laid by ships or aircraft. Unlike the contact mines, these were cylindrical in shape and when dropped by an aircraft were parachuted down. At first, aircraft had to fly low in order to drop these mines but the use of radar aboard the aircraft meant that later mines could be dropped accurately from as high as 15,000 feet (4,572m). The United States, United Kingdom and Germany were the main users of influence mines as the Soviet Union did not have these until 1943 and the Japanese only ever had a small number of those captured.

What the British described as land mines were, in fact, sea mines dropped by the Luftwaffe onto British cities. These are covered above in Chapter 8 under 'Bomb Disposal'.

The magnetic mine had been developed in both the UK and Germany but while the Germans resumed development in the 1930s, the British concentrated on countermeasures. As a result, the British were caught off guard when the Germans started laying them in September 1939, initially causing heavy losses. This mine-laying was stopped between December 1939 and March 1940 and when it resumed not enough mines were laid to have a serious impact on British shipping. Meanwhile, in November 1939, the Royal Navy had found a German magnetic mine intact on the banks of the River Thames and by the middle of the following year had developed a magnetic sweep. Magnetic sweeps forced the Germans to switch to acoustic mines but by November 1940, the British had introduced acoustic sweeps that magnified sounds.

A variety of ships were used to sweep mines including specialized warships, some of which doubled up as sloops, and converted merchant vessels and fishing boats. Magnetic mines were destroyed by using a wooden vessel that towed a magnetic sweep known as the 'LL', consisting of two long insulated and buoyant cables with a strong electric current run through them to create a magnetic field that detonated the mines. Sometimes magnetic coils on wooden barges were used, as were low-flying aircraft with large circular magnetic coils. Most effective of all was degaussing, which neutralized the magnetism of a steel hull by discharging an electric current through a copper cable wrapped around its hull. This process had to be repeated at regular intervals. So important was this that even after the war, for many years the British government paid ship-owners to have degaussing fitted to their ships.

Pressure mines came towards the end of the war in 1944. These were first introduced by the Germans and code-named 'Oyster' by the Allies. The Germans had invented this type of mine earlier in the war but did not use it for fear that the Allies would again discover one and copy it, using it against them on inland waterways and in the shallow waters of the Baltic where such a mine would be most effective. With the magnetic and acoustic mines, the Germans had rushed to deploy them as soon as they were available, which meant that they were countered before they could inflict sufficient damage. Holding back the deployment of the pressure mine meant that they were able to drop more than 400 off the coast of Normandy. Heavy losses were inflicted on Allied shipping before one such mine was recovered and dismantled. Through trial and error, the British were able to estimate the maximum speed at which a ship could move in different depths of water without triggering the device but no effective countermeasure was ever devised.

Post-war, mine countermeasures remained important, especially as most Soviet warships had mine-laying capability. Improved sonars meant that mine-hunters worked in conjunction with minesweepers and later hunter-sweepers became commonplace. Many post-war minesweepers were of wooden construction to reduce the dangers of magnetic mines. In the 1980s, glass-reinforced plastic was used to provide the same benefits but with significantly reduced maintenance costs. The British Hunt-class ships proved expensive to build and were soon joined by the cheaper *Sandown* class.

Mine countermeasures have also changed. With magnetic, acoustic and pressure mines more usual than the moored contact mine, remotely-controlled submersibles are now used. When a sonar seems to have detected a mine, this is investigated by the submersible: its operator is able to see the mine on a screen aboard the mine countermeasures vessel (MCMV) and if a mine is discovered, the submersible lays an explosive charge before withdrawing to a safe distance to detonate the charge and the mine. British *Sandown*-class MCMVs have sonar that can detect objects on the sea bed at a distance of more than 3,280 feet (1,000m).

The major navies all have mine countermeasures vessels, with those of the Western allies concerned that terrorists could lay mines at vulnerable and strategically-important shipping lanes such as the Straits of Hormuz, which connect the Persian Gulf and the Gulf of Oman and through which much of the world's oil passes.

Chapter 29

Air Defence Ships

It became obvious that ships were vulnerable to aerial attack even during the First World War and in the immediate post-war years trials were carried out with aircraft using bombs and torpedoes against warships. Bombing a warship in port was relatively easy but a ship under way was a different matter, as in the time taken between the bombs being released and falling to the level of the target, the ship could take evasive action. Dive-bombing was far more successful, as proved on a number of occasions and especially at the Battle of Midway in June 1942. Better still was the torpedo-bomber, for as one American admiral put it: 'It is easier to get water into a ship from the bottom than from the top!'

None of these methods of sinking a ship using aircraft was easy. Bombs could, and did, bounce off the armoured decks and the turrets containing the main armament of battleships, or the bombs could even break up. Dropping a torpedo into the sea was also difficult, as if dropped too high or at too high a speed, it too could break up. Drop it too far from the target and it could run out of compressed air and stop short of the target. Dive-bombing was an art. The pilot had to know when to pull back and release the bomb, hoping to be able to clear the target ship with its often tall superstructure. The altimeter was of little use in a steep dive as it could not unwind fast enough to give an accurate reading. If a plane was too high, it was likely to miss the target but if it was too low the bomb might not have time to prime itself before hitting the ship or the resulting explosion could take the aircraft with it, as happened on the Arctic convoy PQ18 when the munitions ship SS *Mary Luckenbach* blew up, taking a Luftwaffe aircraft with her.

Skilled ships' masters and commanding officers would always try to 'comb' a torpedo, hoping to steer the ship so that torpedoes passed by harmlessly.

Despite these problems, many ships were sunk by aircraft during the Second World War and others damaged badly enough for surface vessels to finish them off, as in the hunt for the German battleship *Bismarck*. The most spectacular attack against a ship was that of RAF Bomber Command's Nos. 9 and 617 Squadrons against the German battleship

Tirpitz, sitting in a Norwegian fjord which gave it the advantage of forcing attacking aircraft to fly high. The squadrons used 12,000lb Tallboy bombs, also known as 'earthquake' bombs, which capsized the ship.

The British had a narrow escape when the fast armoured aircraft carrier HMS *Illustrious* was bombed off Malta in January 1940 and bombs blew in her aircraft lifts. She was badly damaged but survived. The Royal Navy knew that had another carrier, HMS *Ark Royal*, been attacked with such force, she would have been lost.

Recognizing the need for strong anti-aircraft defence for the fleet and for ships in convoys, before the war the Royal Navy had begun to convert light cruisers dating from the First World War into anti-aircraft ships. The First World War light cruiser was far smaller than its late 1930s equivalent and this was a means of ensuring that these ships continued to provide useful service. These were the C-class cruisers, all built between 1917 and 1919 and originally intended to be scrapped under the London Naval Treaty of 1930. In 1935 the decision was taken to convert all of these ships, replacing all 6-inch and 3-inch guns and the torpedo tubes with ten high-angle 4-inch guns in single mountings. Some of them had multi-barrelled pom-pom guns, firing 2lb shells and known as 'Chicago pianos' to those aboard the ships, and which many naval personnel maintained were the best anti-aircraft weapon the Royal Navy had during the war. Removing the original main and secondary armaments meant that the ships had to be ballasted to maintain stability. These vessels were an invaluable addition to the fleet but no fewer than five of them were sunk on operations; one by a submarine and the rest by enemy aircraft.

As the war progressed, all warships saw their anti-aircraft armament being increased. Some, especially in the Pacific theatre, had little free deck space left and upper decks were frequently jammed with a long line of anti-aircraft weapons, especially once the *kamikaze* suicide aircraft attacks began.

While the innovations of the war such as the corvette and the return of the frigate to the Royal Navy were mainly concerned with anti-submarine warfare, anti-aircraft armament was never neglected. The Loch-class frigates, intended as improved convoy escorts, were followed by a development, almost a sub-class, designated the Bay class. The latter differed in that they had a heavier AA armament for service in the Far East.

The frigate had been an important part of the Royal Navy, as well as other navies, in Nelson's day. It was a general-purpose ship that did much of the work, with the large ships of the line, predecessors of the battleship, only coming together for major fleet engagements. The type had fallen out of use and by the start of the Second World War, the frigate's successor was the destroyer. Its return was due to the need for something larger and more capable than a corvette, mainly for convoy escort duties.

Post-war frigates were mainly specialized anti-submarine or anti-aircraft types, although the Royal Navy did have a small number of air-craft direction frigates. Initially the post-war frigate was generally a slower ship than the destroyer, with the latter having up to eight 4.5-inch guns in four turrets. During the mid-1950s, this began to change. The general-purpose frigate emerged, first with the *Whitby* class and then its successor the *Rothesay* class, the former designed to accommodate a helicopter, with a landing platform and a hangar. In the next few years, the guided missile destroyer made its appearance with the County class: far larger than any destroyer to date and indeed heavier, at more than 5,000 tons stan-dard displacement, than a First World War light cruiser. This led many to describe the ships as cruisers, despite having 'D' for destroyer pennant numbers and 4.5-inch guns. This was the start of a role-reversal between frigates and destroyers, as the guided missiles carried were Sea Slug long-range surface-to-air missiles. Frigates had the shorter-range but highly successful Sea Cat SAM, as well as Limbo depth-charge mortars.

Following on from the *Rothesay* class was what many regard as being one of the finest general-purpose frigates of all time, the *Leander* class, which was also the last British warship class to be ordered in reasonable numbers with a total of twenty-six being built. Their design was also adopted by the Royal Netherlands Navy. The last steam turbine British warships, the *Leander* class also had Sea Cat surface-to-air missiles but on most of the class these were later replaced by Sea Wolf SAMs, while Exocet anti-ship missiles were later added on modernization and the Limbo anti-submarine mortars replaced by twin triple anti-submarine torpedoes. The helicopter eventually employed was the Westland Naval Lynx, replacing the earlier Westland Wasp.

The 1970s saw the Type 42 destroyer, also known as the *Sheffield* class after the lead ship HMS *Sheffield*, join the Royal Navy, with Sea Dart SAMs that could change targets after launch and also had a secondary surface-to-surface capability. The weakness of this class was the absence of any close-in defence system against low-flying aircraft or guided missiles, something cruelly brought home to the Royal Navy when the lead ship of the class and another ship, HMS *Coventry*, were both sunk during the Falklands campaign of 1982. This was a timely reminder that the defen-sive armament of too many British warships had been scaled back too dramatically, resulting in many ships being hastily refitted with improved anti-aircraft and anti-missile defences. These were mainly gun-based with such weapons as the Dutch 'Goalkeeper', a seven-barrelled gun capable of firing 4,200 rounds per minute, and the American 'Phalanx', a 20mm Gatling gun capable of firing 3,000 rounds per minute and with a range of up to 1 mile (1.6km). Other navies have followed the same course. The Type 23 frigates used Sea Wolf SAMs from the start but for the first time instead of using launchers, vertical-launch versions were used, all based in a deck silo able to accommodate thirty-two missiles. Sea Dart missile-launchers on the Royal Navy's *Invincible*-class aircraft carriers were replaced with Phalanx or Goalkeeper close-in gun systems.

The latest class of warship to join the Royal Navy is the Type 45 *Daring*-class destroyer, designed for anti-aircraft and anti-missile warfare using the Sea Viper PAAMS (Principal Anti Air Missile System). Built to replace the Type 42 destroyers that had served during the Falklands War, the British National Audit Office reported that during an intensive attack a single Type 45 could simultaneously track, engage and destroy more targets than five Type 42 destroyers operating together.

Chapter 30

Anti-Submarine Warfare

Despite extensive use of the submarine in the First World War in which the Royal Navy conducted successful campaigns in the Baltic and the Bosphorus and German U-boats at one time brought the United Kingdom to the brink of starvation, anti-submarine warfare in 1939 was not much further forward in most navies than it had been in 1918. One of the few exceptions was the Royal Navy which had sonar, then known as ASDIC (see Introduction). ASDIC used sound echoes to detect a submarine with the sound bouncing off the hull of the submarine. This was a massive improvement over the hydrophones used during the war that detected the sound of a submarine but with reception being adversely affected by the sound of the machinery and propellers of the ship using the equipment.

Without a means of detection, the only way of attacking a submarine was for the submarine-hunter to track back along the wake of the torpedo before casting depth-charges over the side in the hope that the submarine would still be close enough to be damaged. When Japan entered the Second World War in December 1941, this was the only means of anti-submarine warfare available to the Imperial Japanese Navy.

In fact, the effectiveness of ASDIC or sonar was overestimated, especially by the Germans. Admiral Raeder, head of the *Kriegsmarine* (German navy), disagreed strongly with his senior submarine officer, Dönitz, arguing that the use of sonar made U-boat operations hazardous and that these were likely to be of short duration before they had to be suspended. However, Dönitz's faith in his U-boats was to be justified, as events proved.

Sonar had its weaknesses, some of which persist to this day. In colder waters with layers of different temperatures and sometimes of different density with cold fresh glacial water mixing with sea water, as off Norway and Iceland, the sonar pulses could be distorted. It could only provide the distance and direction of a submarine, so depth-charges had to be set to explode at different depths. There was also a blank spot when the submarine passed under the vessel using the sonar, known as 'deaf time' and extending to up to the final 600 feet (183m) or so of the run over the target.

Deaf times and the time taken for depth-charges to sink offered experienced submarine commanders precious seconds in which to take evasive action.

There were many ways of destroying a submarine, which were as vulnerable as any other form of vessel to mines, and many mines were laid at a depth which meant that they were intended specifically for submarines. It is generally believed that a third of the Royal Navy's submarine losses during the Second World War were due to enemy mines. Only one British submarine, HMS *Triumph*, survived hitting a mine, struck while running on the surface in the middle of the night, and her survival was all the more incredible as her torpedo tubes, fully-loaded, were blown off. A strong pressure wave passed down the submarine as a result of the explosion while the crew were having their main meal of the day and it was noted that 'some soup was spilt'.

Other destructive means included torpedoes from other submarines, which is probably how HMS *Upholder* was lost in the Mediterranean. If caught on the surface, gunfire and bombs also accounted for many submarines, therefore submarine commanders were careful not to spend too much time on the surface. The main German submarine bases in France and Heligoland were constructed of strong ferro-concrete, invulnerable to bombs until the arrival of the earthquake bombs later in the war which destroyed these structures by landing alongside and burrowing into the ground before exploding and destroying the foundations so that the submarine pen collapsed. Prior to this, ordinary bombs simply bounced off.

If on the surface, submarines were vulnerable to attack by surface vessels, other submarines and, of course, maritime-reconnaissance aircraft. The need to surface daily to recharge batteries usually meant surfacing at night. Later German electro-submarines only needed to recharge their batteries every two or three days but these entered service in very small numbers and too late to have an impact on the outcome of the war. Aircraft could use bombs but depth-charges were preferred in case the submarine dived. Some German submarine commanders preferred to stay on the surface and fight, as later German U-boats had much-enhanced anti-aircraft gunnery, usually aft of the conning tower, at some cost in submerged speed because of the drag of the extra armament. Nevertheless, submarines that remained on the surface when attacked by an aircraft sometimes won.

The need to surface to recharge batteries was ended with the introduction of the *Schnorchel* ('snorkel'), the name being German slang for nose, changed to snorkel by the Americans and by the British to 'snork'. The British Admiralty had been offered this Dutch invention in 1940 and rejected it. The device was a combined air intake and diesel exhaust outlet. However, remaining submerged was not always a guarantee of escaping detection as apart from ASDIC, aircraft began to be fitted with air-to-surface vessel (ASV) radar or the American equivalent ASH (air-to-surface H), and this even included the otherwise antiquated Fairey Swordfish biplane. As these radars developed, they could spot a snorkel or raised periscope from some distance. Some submarines were fitted with upward-facing periscopes that could spot an aircraft but usually the balance of surprise lay with the aircraft. At night, centimetric radar and a good air-borne searchlight proved an effective combination.

Even when completely submerged and with no visible clues on the surface such as a periscope or snorkel to betray their presence, technology was outpacing the submarine. The Americans developed the magnetic anomaly detector (MAD), which located submerged submarines by noting their localized impact on the earth's magnetic field and the first successful use of this was when a Consolidated Catalina flying boat sunk a submerged U-boat in the Strait of Gibraltar in 1944.

Depth-charges were not the most effective anti-submarine weapon as they had to be pre-set to explode at a certain depth and if they exploded too far above or below a submarine, they risked failing to sink it. Submarines were sometimes blown apart by depth-charges but more usually the depth-charge created so much 'over-pressure' that the submarine's hull could not withstand it and imploded. At first, depth-charges were simply dropped over the stern of the submarine-hunters but these ships had to be moving at a reasonable speed, otherwise they risked having their sterns blown off when the depth-charge exploded.

Depth-charges were fairly similar in all navies, although they varied in size. They consisted of strong canisters filled with high explosive, varying in weight from 198lb to 300lb (90kg to 136kg), although those for small patrol craft were lighter, and actuated by a hydrostatic device at depth, which in the case of the British Mk VII Heavy could be as deep as 850 feet (259m) and which had an effective lethal range of just under 30 feet (9m). Depth-charges dropped by aircraft had stabilizing fins. Surface vessels would usually drop depth-charges in patterns to increase their chances of one exploding close enough to a submarine and typically would drop five at once in what was known as the 'Five of Clubs' pattern, with three being rolled over the rails at the stern and one on either quarter being despatched by throwers. Lighter and heavier depth-charges could be mixed in a pattern, with the heavier ones sinking more quickly. Even if a submarine was not destroyed, it could be damaged or forced so deep that it no longer posed a threat.

Only the Allies managed to tackle 'deaf time' satisfactorily. The solution was to develop weapons that could fire anti-submarine weapons ahead of the ship. The British developed the Hedgehog, which was adopted by the United States navy who preferred it to the smaller Mousetrap. Hedgehog fired twenty-four light projectiles mounted on six rows of spigots, with the rows tilted to compensate for the rolling motion of the ship and each individual spigot angled to spread the projectiles over a circular area some 130 feet (40m) in diameter. One drawback was that the projectiles only exploded on contact with a submarine, so did not have the value of forcing it to go deeper.

Bringing the effectiveness of both conventional depth-charge attack and forward throwing was the Squid, which first appeared in 1943 and was used only by the British. This was a triple-barrelled mortar that fired projectiles containing 200lb of Minol II, a powerful explosive, and sank nearly three times faster than a depth-charge, exploding at an automatically-set depth in triangular patterns with 120-foot (36m) sides. Using double mountings known as Double Squid produced two depth layers almost 60 feet (18m) apart. These devices increased the probability of destroying a submarine from 6 per cent with depth-charges and 20 per cent with Hedgehog to 50 per cent. Nevertheless, it is estimated that 43 per cent of all German submarines were destroyed using depth-charges.

Anti-submarine operations frequently saw aircraft and ships working together and this cooperation often proved to be highly efficient.

Post-War
Anti-submarine warfare had made such strides forward during the Second World War that post-war progress slowed and the systems evolved during the war remained adequate. The ships and aircraft improved but the main means of destroying a submarine remained the depth-charge. Nevertheless, the new Limbo triple-barrelled depth-charge launcher was placed at the stern of frigates. The only significant post-war class to have forward-firing launchers was the Royal Navy's *Blackwood*-class frigates, which had two forward-firing triple-barrelled launchers in place of what would have been 'A' turret, the forward gun mounting.

Changes were in hand, none the less. By the beginning of the 1960s, frigates and destroyers were being fitted with hangars and landing-platforms for helicopters capable of carrying an anti-submarine torpedo. Torpedo tubes also made a comeback on these two types of warship, not to deliver the *coup de grâce* to a damaged enemy capital ship, but to sink submarines.

Many navies placed much faith in using guided missiles to drop torpedoes or depth-charges that were parachuted down to the surface of the sea, the two prime types being the Australian Ikara and the American ASROC (Anti-Submarine ROCket). These missiles enabled the torpedo or depth-charge to be carried between 2,000 and 10,000 yards (1,830 to 9,144m) to the area in which the submarine was believed to be positioned, within minutes. The advantage was that torpedoes had a very limited range and using the guided missile extended this by several times. The Royal Navy retrofitted Ikara to some of its *Leander*-class frigates, while others received Exocet surface-to-surface missiles and two triple anti-submarine torpedo tubes.

The use of missiles to speed the delivery of anti-submarine torpedoes or depth-charges had competition, however, from the increasingly capable helicopter. The Sikorsky S-58, also built under licence as the Westland Wessex, carried its own dunking sonar so that the helicopter could hover and listen for submarines before unleashing an anti-submarine torpedo. The dunking sonabuoy naturally gave the helicopter's presence away, so a system of passive sonars known as 'Jezebel' was devised. These could be dropped by helicopters or maritime-reconnaissance aircraft without the submarine being able to detect their presence and the sonabuoys were dropped in a pattern that enabled a fix to be made on the submarine's position. This was then transmitted to the helicopter or aircraft so that a homing torpedo could be dropped as close as possible to the target. However, one weakness of the dropped sonabuoy was that these could seldom be recovered, making the system extremely expensive in use.

The increasing size and speed of submarines, as well as the greater operational depths, all made possible by nuclear propulsion, meant that methods had to be revised as a submarine could race out of range before a torpedo could catch it and conventional depth-charges were of little use. The answer was to use nuclear depth-charges or 'depth-bombs' that could not only sink very quickly but could also produce sufficient over-pressure to destroy any submarine within a wide radius.

While nuclear submarines are associated in the public mind with ballistic missile-carrying types, most nuclear submarines are what might be described as 'hunter-killers' or, in the Royal Navy, fleet submarines. They are designed to carry out a wide range of duties including countering enemy submarines, of which the most important are, of course, those carrying ballistic missiles or, increasingly, nuclear-tipped cruise missiles.

Additionally, the problems of temperature layers in the water affecting sonar have now been countered to some extent by the use of variable-depth sonars in anti-submarine warships.

Chapter 31

Containers

Today, most general cargo moved by sea is carried within a container and ships with upwards of 1,000 containers are not uncommon. Containers not only protect the cargo but just as importantly cargo-handling is mechanized, thereby improving productivity and lowering costs, while the widespread availability of road-haulage vehicles and railway wagons able to carry containers means that little time is lost in transhipment. The fact that containers can be stacked also means that dockside warehousing is no longer required.

Various forms of container have existed for many centuries, with some suggesting that the *amphorae* used by the ancient Greeks were a form of container. Indeed they were, but manhandling of goods was still necessary. The appearance of the railways eventually saw a form of container that could be moved by crane from railway wagon to delivery vehicle and back again but these could not be stacked. For the railways, the growth in such containers took place mainly between 1920 and 1939. The rate of growth was faster in the United Kingdom than in the United States where railway companies expected customers to deliver freight to the goods yards and then take it away when it arrived by rail, while in the UK the railway companies saw collection and delivery as part of their business. The largest British railway company, the London, Midland and Scottish, had just 400 containers in 1926 but by 1933 it had 3,713 and on nationalization in 1948 more than half the 19,358 containers inherited by British Railways came from the LMS. Nevertheless, these were non-stackable and often built of wood.

Some of the first wartime usage of containers came with the Australian army, whose efficiency was hampered by the lack of a national standard railway track gauge across the country. To counter this, the Australian army used containers but they were still of the non-stackable variety.

As the Second World War reached its end, the United States army used specialized containers known as 'transporters' to speed the loading and unloading of transport ships. Apart from moving military stores, these were initially seen as a secure and efficient means of shipping the household goods of officers in the field. As with the railway containers, these were reusable but for the first time the containers were built of rigid steel. Their use continued during the Korean War for moving sensitive military equipment, while thefts from wooden containers and the damage these suffered during transhipment also underlined the need to use rigid steel.

It was not until 1952 that the US army standardized the dimensions of containers to 8 feet high by 8 feet wide and 10, 20, 30 or 40-foot lengths. These measurements were later taken as standard by the International Standards Organization (ISO) but first an increase in height to 8 feet 6 inches was approved, followed by a further increase to 9 feet and now 9 feet 6 inch containers are available. The carrying capacity of container ships is expressed in 20-foot equivalent units or TEUs and some of the more modern ships can carry more than 14,000 TEUs, which usually means more than 7,000 40-foot units. In the meantime, the corner fitments of containers were also standardized to ensure that container-handling equipment and stacking is the same worldwide. The United States was the first country to allow containers to be double-stacked, i.e. two containers high, on railway wagons.

Bibliography

Most books on the Second World War deal with one aspect, perhaps air, land or sea, or a particular theatre of war, and there are relatively few books dealing with the war as a whole. For convenience, titles are listed here as in the book in terms of general, air, land or sea warfare.

General
Dear, I.C.B. and Foot, M.R.D., *The Oxford Companion to the Second World War* (Oxford, Oxford University Press, 1995)
Downing, Taylor and Johnston, Andrew, *Battle Stations: Decisive Weapons of the Second World War* (Barnsley, Pen & Sword, 2000)
Keegan, John, *Encyclopaedia of World War II* (London, Hamlyn, 1977)

Air
Collier, Basil, *History of Air Power* (London, Weidenfeld & Nicolson, 1974)
Jane's Fighting Aircraft of World War II, Foreword by Bill Gunston (London, Random House, 2001)
Piekalkiewicz, Janusz, *The Air War: 1939–1945* (London, Blandford, 1985)
Wragg, David, *Royal Air Force Handbook 1939–1945* (Stroud, The History Press, 2007)

Land
Haskew, Michael E., *Encyclopedia of Elite Forces in the Second World War* (Barnsley, Pen & Sword, 2007)
Kennedy, Paul, *Engineers of Victory: The Problem-Solvers Who Turned the Tide in the Second World War* (London, Allen Lane, 2013)
Millett, Alan and Williamson, Murray, *Military Effectiveness* (London, Allen & Unwin, 1987)

Sea
Ireland, Bernard, *Jane's Naval History of World War II* (London, HarperCollins, 1998)
Mallmann Showell, Jak P., *German Navy Handbook 1939–1945* (Stroud, The History Press, 1999)
Preston, Antony, *Destroyers* (London, Bison, 1978)
Wragg, David, *Royal Navy Handbook 1939–1945* (Stroud, The History Press, 2005)

Index